BLOW YOUR OWN HORN!

Personal Branding for Business Professionals

RAE A. STONEHOUSE

Copyright © 2020 by Rae A. Stonehouse.

All rights reserved.

No part of this book may be reproduced in any form or by any electronic or mechanical means, including information storage and retrieval systems, without written permission from the author, except for the use of brief quotations in a book review.

E-book - ISBN: 978-1-7771565-0-3
Print - ISBN: 978-1-7771565-1-0
Live For Excellence Productions
1221 Velrose Drive
Kelowna, B.C., Canada
V1X6R7
https://liveforexcellence.com

❦ Created with Vellum

INTRODUCTION

There's an old saying that goes "the squeaky wheel... gets the grease."

The saying may have been true at one point in time but now...

The business world is a busy and crowded place. How can a business professional standout from the cacophony of others clambering for attention and recognition?

In this world of digital technology, a world where we are as close as 3° of separation to almost anybody in the world, many so-called technological gurus would have us believe we can easily create an on-line persona, a digital makeover if you will.

I would agree with the statement, to a certain extent. It seems daily we hear of fake restaurant or book reviews. We hear of identity theft where unscrupulous characters have stolen someone's ID for fraudulent purposes by creating false identities from what they are able to gather from public sources.

If it is so easy for someone to create these bogus on-line identities, how can we then trust any self-promotional material we view on-line?

INTRODUCTION

I believe creating your on-line persona is important however, it is but one step at a self-promotional and marketing strategy.

This book offers a collection of strategies to build your on-line presence and gain recognition in your community.

Your goal may be to raise your prominence at work to apply for a job you have been eying. Perhaps, your goal is to run for political office, but it seems no one knows who you are. You may be like me, an authorpreneur wanting to promote my publications, myself as an author and my self-publishing business.

You can be brilliant in what you do. If you are a well kept secret, you are not helping yourself or your clients. As an author, you need to put your body of work out there. Articles, blogs and podcasts come into play. We talk about them later in the book.

By putting your ideas out there it does three things:

1) It really builds your credibility as a subject matter expert in that area.

2) It creates/reinforces your brand equity, your value in the marketplace.

3) It creates market gravity... some might call market pull.

If you aren't an author... well then perhaps you should be. We all have expertise that could be in demand by those who don't and are willing to pay you for your advice.

Self-promotion hasn't come easily to me.

As a shy introvert, I believed if I had done something praiseworthy the people in the position to deliver the praise would know and I shouldn't have to draw it to their attention.

As a registered nurse I recall working on a project with another nurse. I did most of the research and put the project report together. She did

INTRODUCTION

very little to participate however, upon completion, she took all the credit.

Back about 20 years or so ago I had an experience that awakened me to the value of self-promotion and the negative consequences of not doing so.

I was contemplating enrolling in a university program focused on leadership, training and organizational development. The program was designed for adult learners and was granting credit towards life and experiential lessons.

I had lots of experience to leverage and the skills to successfully complete the course. Where I fell short was in being able to provide testimonials as to my personal characteristics and my strengths and weaknesses.

I had my personal references lined up. That was easy, I had fellow workers and members of community organizations I was involved with, who provided me with testimonials.

The problem arose from not having a work-based manager or employer to provide a testimonial for me. As a worker, I tended to have as little as possible to do with my supervisors as I could. I did my job and did little over and above my duties. This meant I didn't have anybody to provide a supervisor-employee testimonial.

How could they?

They didn't know me. They didn't know what I was capable of, how could they possibly recommend me?

This was enlightening. It challenged my usual way of thinking. If I was to get ahead in the world, I needed to be able to learn how to leverage my relationships. When I say leverage, I don't necessarily mean to exploit them. I see value in developing mutually beneficial relationships which can lead to win-win results.

As I was contemplating this challenge of not having a supervisor's testimonial there was a change in our provincial government. I live in

INTRODUCTION

British Columbia, Canada. The new government significantly increased the cost of tuition for the program. It went from an affordable $8500 for a two-year program to over $22,000. This effectively closed the window of opportunity for me.

Fast forward a few years or so, actually more than a decade to be honest. I found myself as a director for a local society supporting entrepreneurs. At this point I had been a Toastmaster member for a decade or so and was used to organizing meetings and promoting Toastmaster's events. With my event organizing experience, I took on the role of VP Training & Development. My role was to organize our monthly town hall meetings where we showcased local entrepreneurial sage experts and allowed them to share their skills and experiences with fellow entrepreneurs.

In that capacity, I stretched the boundaries of what would normally be considered an event organizer. I developed the topics. I created the marketing promotion. I added the promotional copy to our website and then created and monitored the on-line event registration system.

If that wasn't enough, I recruited our panelists and worked with them to develop promotional material about themselves, which I added to our website for event promotion. I then developed the discussion questions that would be asked to the panelists as I was also the moderator for the panel discussion.

I organized some 30 of these town halls over a period of 2 years. At the same time I was developing websites which involved considerable promotional copywriting.

Writing promotional copy for these events and to promote the speakers for those events, raised my promotional skills significantly.

I learned it's far easier to promote someone else, that is their strengths, their skills, their experiences than it was to promote myself.

As I think back to my journey of self-promotion it may have started with delivering Toastmasters speeches. Part of delivering an effective speech is providing an introduction for your introducer to introduce

INTRODUCTION

you to your audience. Your introduction should grab your audience's attention, so they are eager to hear what you have to say.

Your introduction should also set up your credibility so it answers the question that most of the audience members are asking themselves "why should I listen to this speaker?"

In developing your introduction, you are providing the introducer the promotional copy you have crafted. Instead of 'blowing your own horn', which would've happened if it were you introducing yourself, it becomes more powerful if somebody else is saying these kind words about you. Sure, you wrote them in the first place, but having somebody else say the words makes it more effective in setting you up as somebody worth listening to.

Fast-forward a few more years and I created and operated an on-line community business events calendar. In that capacity, I researched and curated all local business events. I posted these business-related events to my on-line calendar and added promotional copy where needed. I had created some 2000 or more local on-line event listings.

In addition, I created and sent out a weekly newsletter letting people know about the upcoming local business events and promoting events I was interested in or involved with.

At the time of writing this chapter and book, I have written and self-published a dozen or so books in the self-help genre. As an authorpreneur it's necessary to self-promote my books, my self-publishing business and myself as an author. It gets easier the more I do it.

Blow Your Own Horn: Personal Branding for Business Professionals has been a side project for me while I have been working on creating and publishing my other self-help books. As I was writing those books it frequently occurred to me the content I was writing applied to not only the content of that particular book but also applied to the concept of self-promoting.

As we work our way through this book, I have utilized content from my other books to illustrate the point I want to make.

INTRODUCTION

Many business professionals are quite comfortable at networking and self-promotion. Many of us aren't and may find it more painful than pleasurable. I've written this book from the perspective of having been a once shy introvert who has learned to become less shy and how to self-promote effectively on my journey through life.

If I can do it... you can do it too.

This book is for business professionals who want to raise their visibility in a crowded workplace or a personal interest venture.

Some will tell you blowing your own horn is bragging. I forward an argument against that belief in an upcoming chapter.

Others will tell you promoting yourself requires you to be phony or to be someone you really aren't.

If we are to move forward and benefit from our accomplishments, we need to self-promote.

Kurt Vonnegut, with his dry wit, knew better. "We are what we pretend to be, so we must be careful what we pretend to be," he wrote in Mother Night (1961).

Perhaps Vonnegut hit the proverbial nail in the head... "we are pretending..."

"Fake it until you make it" is an old saying that readily comes to mind. While you are faking it, you are developing skills that will eventually allow you to make it... without faking it.

If you want people to toot your horn, you have to provide them with the info you want them to promote. This is not a passive activity. You need to take the initiative to train your trumpeters so their message is favorable. Of equal importance, is tooting other people's horns. Fair is fair.

As in other books I have written I use what I call the "onion" method

INTRODUCTION

of writing. We'll take a close look at one layer at a time until we have a good understanding of our subject. Each content topic is stand-alone and it isn't necessary to complete the previous one before working on the steps of another.

I've divided this book up into parts to look at personal branding and marketing from different perspectives.

Firstly, we look at personal branding and marketing.

Secondly, we look at self-promotion utilizing Linkedin as a tool.

Then we look at effective networking techniques for self-promotion.

The Networking Section is followed by self-promotion strategies related to job searching.

After the Self-Promotion When Job Searching Section we look at on-line reputation management and additional social media venues that could be helpful to you in developing your personal brand.

We close our exploration of self-promotional strategies with Resource files to add to our understanding of the topic.

At the end of many of the chapters you will find a list of *Action Items* for you to complete that will help you move forward in developing your self-promotional skills.

Developing any new skill requires a change of your mindset.

Here is a poem I found years ago that I like to refer to often.

If you always think

The way you have always thought

You will always feel

The way you have always felt

And

If you always feel

INTRODUCTION

The way you have always felt

You will always do

What you have always done

And

If you always do

What you have always done

You will always get

What you have always gotten

If there is no change

There is no change

Author Unknown

In our next chapter we explore the concept of personal branding, what it really means, why we should do it and what often prevents us from doing it.

PART I
PERSONAL BRANDING & MARKETING

PERSONAL BRANDING

In this Chapter we explore the concept of personal branding, what it really means, why we should do it and what often prevents us from doing it.

If you Google your name, what comes up?

If the answer is "nothing", you probably haven't spent much time developing your personal brand.

So, what is personal branding?

According to Wikipedia, *personal branding* is the practice of people marketing themselves and their careers as *brands*.

It's probably a good idea to determine what a *brand* is before moving on.

Once again from Wikipedia...

A *brand* is a name, term, design, symbol, or other feature that distinguishes one seller's product from those of others.

Brands are used in business, marketing and advertising.

A brand is any name, design, style, words or symbols used singularly or in combination that distinguishes one product from another in the eyes of the customer.

Branding is a set of marketing and communication methods that help to distinguish a company from competitors and create a lasting impression in the minds of customers.

The key components that form a brand's toolbox include a brand's identity, brand communication (such as by logos and trademarks), brand awareness, brand loyalty and various brand management strategies.

We are all familiar with commercial branding and are likely bombarded with it every day. Coca Cola, Pepsi Cola and Nike readily come to mind.

These are well-established brands.

Now back to the idea of *personal* branding...

While previous self-help management techniques were about self-improvement, the personal-branding concept suggests instead that success comes from self-packaging.

The term is thought to have been first used and discussed in a 1997 article by Tom Peters.

Personal branding is essentially the ongoing process of establishing a prescribed image or impression in the mind of others about an individual, group, or organization.

Personal branding often involves the application of one's name to various products.

Athletes and celebrities come to mind.

If that is your situation, well good for you!

I would expect that you have staff to look after you.

For the rest of us mere mortals, let's drill down a little.

Developing a personal brand takes work, and it's not going to happen overnight. But once you do it, the benefits are endless.

In this next section we explore personal branding, what it really means, why we should do it and what often *prevents* us from doing it.

Why Should We Create a Personal Brand?

It Helps You Stand out from the Crowd:

A personal brand is a great way to demonstrate your skills and knowledge about a particular subject or field.

Building a brand is your chance to show your audience what you know and why you know it, and it will help set you apart from others who might be vying for the same opportunities but who haven't taken the time to build their own personal brand.

It Leads to Opportunities:

A strong personal brand can lead to a multitude of opportunities, including:

- Job interviews
- Internships
- Speaking engagements
- Networking opportunities
- Promotions
- Partnerships

A personal brand is the building blocks that will lead to success for your future. It can help you reach any number of goals, both personal and professional, and it can also lead to many opportunities for advancement in your career.

It Inspires Trust in Your Audience:

Many people, especially those of the millennial generation, don't trust larger businesses that utilize traditional advertising.

That's why there's such a big push nowadays to "shop small", and why influencer advertising is so successful.

People are much more likely to buy from, and listen to, someone who looks, talks, and acts like them as opposed to a large corporation.

So if you build your brand like a business, but still maintain a personal front, you're guaranteed to inspire trust amongst your audience.

Someone Is Always Going to Be Screening You On-line:

Whether you're applying for college, for an entry-level job, or for your future career, someone is going to be Googling your name.

Some employers will expect you to have an on-line presence, whereas others just want to ensure you don't have a poor reputation on-line.

Developing a personal brand is a great way to show potential employers that you've worked hard to build a positive reputation on-line.

Source: Search Engine Journal https://www.searchenginejournal.com/what-is-personal-branding-why-important/327367/#close

So why don't we self-promote?

There are numerous reasons many of us don't like to talk about ourselves to others.

Perhaps we were taught at a young age from our mothers that it is wrong to promote yourself?

"It is bragging and nobody likes braggarts!"

That may be a generalization and it really isn't fair to pick on mothers, considering all the good they do for us.

However, while many people likely don't like braggarts, it doesn't necessarily follow that talking about yourself in a favorable light... is bragging.

Are you starting to wonder about the picture illustrated above? His name is Walt Whitman, and he was an American Cowboy poet, essayist and journalist, way back in the mid to later 1800s.

I'm fond of his quote about personal branding.

He probably didn't relate it any way to personal branding but here it goes...

"If you done it... it ain't bragging!"

I think Walt hit the proverbial nail on the head. If you have done something and you talk about it, then it isn't bragging.

That sounds like self-promotion to me.

Can you think of any other reasons we don't self-promote?

It could be a simple matter of we really *don't know how* to promote ourselves.

I'm hoping this book resolves the problem for you if you identify with that reason.

Another simple reason may be we *don't have time* to self-promote.

Throughout this book I provide strategies you will be able to follow and start self-promoting.

Like any other skill development, it takes time and practice to become good at it.

As your skill in self-promotion increases and your self-confidence as well, you should find it easier to self-promote.

Then there is a simple reason that most of us have likely experienced at one time or another.

It can be embarrassing at first *when you create promotional copy*, featuring yourself in a good light.

We will introduce on-line promotion and reputation management in a few chapters.

One of the features of social media platforms is a requirement to create a Bio or a Profile.

While these can be a great opportunity for self-promotion, the first few times can be challenging.

Do you write your promotional copy in the first person as "I did this, this and this..."?

Or do you write it in the 3rd person, "Rae Stonehouse, renowned best-selling author is known for..."?

Okay, so I'm not a best selling-author yet, but I have a head start on promoting it.

A FEW YEARS BACK WHEN I WAS RESEARCHING CONTENT FOR MY E-book **Power Networking for Shy People: Tips & Techniques for Moving from Shy to Sly**, I discovered a book by William Bridges... **Creating You & Company: Learn to think like the CEO of your own company.**

Bridges encourages you to market yourself as if *you* are the company.

He takes the corporate idea of branding and challenges us to apply it to ourselves.

I say "Blow your own horn!"

"If you don't, who will?"

Reading his book helped provide clarity and peace of mind for me.

Rather than feeling like a person with multiple personalities as I will describe later on in the book, it was more like having multiple personas. They are all me, each from a different perspective.

I have worked in mental health for many years and have met a few multiple personalities.

They are good people.

Bridge's book helped me to redefine myself in a new way. "Hello, I'm Rae Stonehouse. I am a nurse entrepreneur and a believer in the Law of Attraction!"

"I am open to the opportunities and abundance that the Universe has to offer me."

I'll leave it as that at for your understanding of who I am.

I have an elevator pitch for each of those personas mentioned above that I use in specific situations.

I will illustrate them in further depth later in this book.

~

ACTION ITEMS:

1. Decide for yourself, why you want to self-promote? What is your purpose and what do you hope to achieve?
2. Start to develop a personal brand. What do you want the public to know about you?
3. Create a list of your notable accomplishments.

In our next Chapter, we explore personal marketing.

~

Keep asking yourself, "What kind of a company would my company be if everyone in it was just like me?" Brian Tracy

"A professional is a person who can do his best at a time when he doesn't particularly feel like it." Alistair Cooke

"Challenge everything you do. Expand your thinking. Refocus your efforts. Rededicate yourself to your future." Patricia Fripp

PERSONAL MARKETING

 e've been talking about personal branding. Closely related to branding is marketing.

MARKETING OVERVIEW:

Marketing, as defined by the American Marketing Association "is the activity, set of institutions, and processes for creating, communicating, delivering, and exchanging offerings that have value for customers, clients, partners, and society at large."

Hmmm. Another definition is: The management process through which goods and services move from concept to the customer. It includes the coordination of four elements called the 4 P's of marketing:

(1) identification, selection and development of a product,

(2) determination of its price,

(3) selection of a distribution channel to reach the customer's place, and

(4) development and implementation of a promotional strategy.

The content in this chapter is excerpted from a book I have under development entitled **Content Marketing Strategies That Work: Book Three in the Successful Self-Publisher Series.**

While it is directed towards authors and content creators, the same principles apply to marketing yourself or your product whatever it may be.

There's an old saying: "Advertising is what you pay for, publicity is what you pray for." It can be said that advertising is paid media, public relations is earned media. With advertising, you tell people how great you are. With publicity, others sing your praises.

Most authors don't have the operational budget to spend on paid advertising. Advertising is expensive. Publicity and public relations, while not necessarily totally free, can have a better return on investment than money spent on advertising. Many people confuse advertising and public relations. This table (below) compares the two.

Advertising	Public Relations
Paid	Earned
Builds exposure	Builds trust
Audience is skeptical	Media gives third-party validation
Guaranteed placement	No guarantee, must persuade media
Competitive creative control	Media controls final version
Ads are mostly visual	PR uses language
More expensive	Less expensive
"Buy this product!"	"This is important!"

Advertising vs Public Relations Comparison Chart

TABLE SOURCE: ROBERT WYNNE

"IF YOU ALWAYS DO WHAT YOU'VE ALWAYS DONE, YOU WILL ALWAYS get what you've always gotten!"

Conventional marketing wisdom says you need to touch your customer 7 to 11 times before they make a purchasing decision.

When it comes to touching our customers, don't take that too literally as it will likely get you in trouble if you were to do so!

In a marketing context, a touch is every time your customer sees or hears a mention of your name or brand.

Touchpoint examples could be your website, a tweet from your Twitter account, a post to your Facebook page or someone else's, a blog post focusing on your topic, a Linkedin post, a poster on the wall of a public place etc. The list goes on and on.

An individual needs to see your name and/or your book title, over and over again before they make a decision to check it out. When they are thinking about your topic, whatever it may be, you want them to be thinking your name.

IN OUR NEXT CHAPTER, WE EXPLORE THE CONCEPT OF IDENTIFYING who we actually are.

WHO ARE YOU?

In this chapter we explore the concept of identifying who we actually are.

Knock knock! Who's there? Rae. Rae who? Exactly...

Rae who?

One of the challenges I find with people who are out there promoting themselves and networking to develop contacts and connections is that of deciding who they *actually* are.

That statement might not have made sense to you.

Having low self-esteem for many years I had challenges in defining, at least to myself, who I actually was.

Traditionally, men tend to introduce themselves in relation to what they do for a living.

"Hello, I'm Rae Stonehouse and I'm a Registered Nurse and I've worked in mental health for over 40 years."

Women, conversely, tend to introduce themselves in relation to their role in life. "I'm Diane and I'm the mother of energetic four-year-old twin boys, my husband is a doctor and... oh... I'm also a nurse."

As I took on more volunteer roles and developed entrepreneurial ventures, my identity became more complicated.

In addition to being a nurse I was also a former Boy Scout Leader; a Toastmasters member and a leader; Chairman of a local non-profit agency to support entrepreneurs; a business owner developing an event planning business; a master of ceremonies; a wedding reception emcee and an independent legal services broker.

Whew! I'm overwhelmed just saying it out loud.

Can you imagine what it would be like on the receiving end of my introductions?

It would take ten minutes or so for me to recite and describe all of them and it often did.

It didn't work for me. It often left my listener overwhelmed and confused. It appeared I lacked focus. And at times I certainly did.

While I may be at the far end of the continuum as to the depth of my identity, take the following as an example of someone on the other end of the identity continuum.

In my seminars I like to provide the example of a housewife returning to the workforce as an example of someone with an identity crisis.

Here's the scenario.

A young woman attends university and obtains an advanced degree in computer technology.

Upon graduation she works for five years and rises to the position of Supervisor in the technology department of a mid-sized company.

In the meantime, she marries and several years into her supervisory role she goes off on maternity leave.

Time passes. She decides to quit her job and stay at home to raise her family.

She has two more children.

More time passes and her youngest child has started in school full-time back in the Fall.

Now that all three of her children are in school throughout the day, she feels she is ready to go back to work.

But *who* is she now?

Is she still the Supervisor of the technology department she worked in?

Can she walk back into that position?

Have there been any changes in the computer technology world in the six years or so since she left the workforce?

If she's not that supervisory person anymore, then who is she?

Is she the person she was *before* she took on the supervisory role?

Possibly, possibly not! She would likely need to undertake considerable upgrading to be competitive in her job search.

Or is her identity now that of a housewife?

If so, how can she leverage being a housewife into her job search?

This is an example of an identity crisis.

In the next section we explore some other identity challenges many people face.

YOU ARE MUCH MORE THAN YOUR JOB, YOUR TITLE OR YOUR ROLE IN your family.

So then... who are you?

You are an amalgamation of *all* your roles in life, your skills, your experiences... the good things and the bad things.

They are all you!

In order to promote yourself, you need to have a good understanding of who you are.

I didn't!

A mentor of mine suggested I perform an exercise to gain a better understanding of who I am.

I've included it as an *Action Item* for this lesson.

I'll talk you through it here.

It's simple at first but becomes more challenging as you delve into the exercise.

On a sheet of paper, create a large letter T. On the top of the left-hand column write the words **My Strengths**.

At the top of the right-hand column write the words **My Perceived Weaknesses**.

[Perceived means these are items you believe you are weak in, not what someone else has said about you.]

Start adding to each column. You may find it helpful to categorize your items into the different roles you have in life, or perhaps different activities you engage in.

As you get into the exercise, it becomes more difficult to identify items to write down. But just when you think you are stuck or finished, a new idea will pop up and off you go.

When I completed this exercise, I had more than a dozen pages of items. I am involved in a lot of different areas and endeavors.

Some I am skilled at.

Some not so much.

The final step is to read through your strengths and perceived weaknesses.

I would suspect you have a lot more strengths identified than weaknesses as they can be somewhat easier to accept.

So how is this exercise helpful to you?

Hopefully, it will provide some clarity for you as to the many roles you take on in life.

It should also illustrate you have a lot of strengths to capitalize on.

Many people fall into the trap of focusing on their short-comings or their perceived weaknesses.

Research shows if you want to become more self-confident in what you do, you would be better to focus on your strengths, making them even stronger.

Many are of the belief you should try to strengthen your weaknesses instead of your strengths.

Once again, the research says 'no.' It provides examples like Bill Gates.

Is he a computer whiz? Most certainly.

Is he an excellent public speaker or presenter? Not so well!

What he has done is to capitalize on his strengths, not focus on his weaknesses.

He can pay people to do whatever he isn't good at.

Many successful people do the same thing.

We may not be able to afford others to do what we aren't so good at, but we can certainly become even better at what we *are* good at.

While we are doing so, there is a high possibility we'll start to get better in areas we haven't been so good at.

Action Items:

1. Complete the Strengths/Perceived Weaknesses Exercise.
2. Upon completion of the Strengths/Perceived Weaknesses Exercise assess your results.
3. Celebrate your strengths!
4. Answer the question... "Who am I?"

In our next chapter we take the information we just learned about ourselves and ask "What do we stand for?"

"It takes a lot of things to prove you are smart, but only one thing to prove you are ignorant." Don Herold

"Do not attempt to do a thing unless you are sure of yourself; but do not relinquish it simply because someone else is not sure of you." Stewart E. White

WHAT DO YOU STAND FOR?

In this chapter we take the information we just learned about ourselves and ask "What do you stand for?"

What Do You Stand For?

If you were asked to describe yourself in one word or perhaps a few, what would they be? If I were to ask a colleague or friend of yours the same question, would they offer the same words as yours?

If I were asked that question 10 to 15 years back I would say I was a *catalyst*. As a nurse therapist I helped my patients and fellow staff to move forward with problems in their lives that were holding them back.

I also believe the words *creative, systematic, organized, loyal* and *persistent* come to mind.

What word would you use to describe yourself?

Quite recently, I learned of an acronym that resonates with me. **H.O.P.E.**

Helping Other People Evolve. As I have recently retired from my nursing job, I'm not serving as a catalyst for my patients anymore but I certainly am in the self-help books I write and publish with the systems and strategies I create. The words I used to describe myself ring true and serve me in helping others evolve.

So what words would you use to describe yourself? Do you *walk* your *talk*? Do others know what you stand for? Have you told them? Maybe you should. That's all part of the blowing your own horn concept.

People aren't mind readers. Sometimes you need to tell them what they should be thinking. That's called *marketing*. It would also likely be a good idea to ask the people in your life what they believe you stand for. That's called *research*. Their answers may surprise you.

I will likely remember for the rest of my days, one example of a person who did not *walk* their *talk*. He was the keynote motivational speaker at a conference I attended and was promoting healthy living, being everything that you could be and leading by example. I observed him later that evening in the hotel's bar, pounding back the liquor and smoking like a chimney.

I think the message here is when you are developing your professional image you need to have it turned on at all times. In small communities, people you network with in business situations will likely encounter you at social get-togethers or at the grocery store.

Action Items:

1. Create a list of words you would use to describe yourself.
2. Answer the question... "What do I stand for?"
3. Ask friends and colleagues in your existing network what words they would use to describe you.
4. Ask your friends and colleagues if they believe that you "walk your talk."
5. If they reply "No, you don't", what will you now do with this information?

In the next chapter we explore LinkedIn as a powerful self-promotion and marketing tool.

∼

"Even though you may want to move forward in your life, you may have one foot on the brakes. In order to be free, we must learn how to let go. Release the hurt. Release the fear. Refuse to entertain your old pain. The energy it takes to hang onto the past is holding you back from a new life. What is it you would let go of today?" Mary Manin Morrissey

"Each one of us has a fire in our heart for something. It's our goal in life to find it and to keep it lit." ---Mary Lou Retton [American Olympic Gymnast]

ARE YOU LINKEDIN?

In this chapter we explore Linkedin as a powerful self-promotion and marketing tool.

ARE YOU LINKEDIN? WELL, YOU SHOULD BE!

LINKEDIN AND THE INTERNET IN GENERAL ARE A BOON TO LEARNING and practicing self-promotional skills. The on-line world is a great leveler when it comes to the shy and introverted vs. the extroverted.

When you are reading text on a website or elsewhere, the personality of the author doesn't usually show. I believe many of my fellow introverts have better computer and technological skills than our extroverted colleagues. I further believe our ability to focus on matters and our preference to work alone works in our favor.

You can research a person you want to connect to without ever having to leave the comfort of your home. Mobile apps on your smart phone also mean you can research somebody when you are out and about.

You don't need to wait until you are in front of your desktop computer or laptop for that matter.

I used to describe Linkedin as being like your resume on steroids. The content I had uploaded to my profile was very much in the curriculum vitae style of a resume. It seemed to go on and on when you were reading it. I had added every notable achievement to my list of accomplishments. The fact I was involved with and had lots of experience from many organizations as well as my professional career as a Registered Nurse, made it confusing.

ACTION ITEMS:

1. If you haven't already, sign up for a free Linkedin account.

In our next chapter we look at Linked in strategies to get the most out of your Linkedin membership.

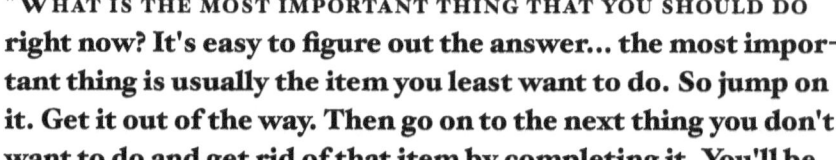

"**What is the most important thing that you should do right now? It's easy to figure out the answer... the most important thing is usually the item you least want to do. So jump on it. Get it out of the way. Then go on to the next thing you don't want to do and get rid of that item by completing it. You'll be amazed at how it frees your spirit not to have them hanging over you." Tom Hopkins**

"**There are four ways, and only four ways, in which we have contact with the world. We are evaluated and classified by these four contacts: what we do, how we look, what we say, and how we say it." Dale Carnegie**

LINKEDIN STRATEGIES FOR PERSONAL BRANDING & MARKETING

In this chapter we explore more strategies to leverage your Linkedin membership for personal branding, self-promotion and marketing.

There are several elements of Linkedin I want to focus on in this chapter that are helpful to a self-promoter.

IT CAN BE YOUR PERSONAL MARKETING AGENCY:

One of the first steps to take after opening your Linkedin account is to start developing your *Profile*. Your profile connects you with others in your Linkedin network. As a new connection is made, often the new contact will go to your profile to learn more about you.

Even people you have known for years will check you out. Imagine the number one thought going through someone's mind as they read your profile is... *"Is there an opportunity for me to do business with this person?"*

Parts of the Profile:

Your Name: You have the option of having your name displayed fully or with your first name and last initial. Example: Rae Stonehouse vs

Rae S. If you are using Linkedin as a business growth strategy, it is suggested you use your full name.

Headline: Provide a descriptive headline statement. It doesn't need to be your current job title, although many people use this field in that way. Something that gives a glimpse into your uniqueness or personality can help you stand out from your competitors.

Here is a headline I used a while back when I was operating a Master of Ceremonies business.

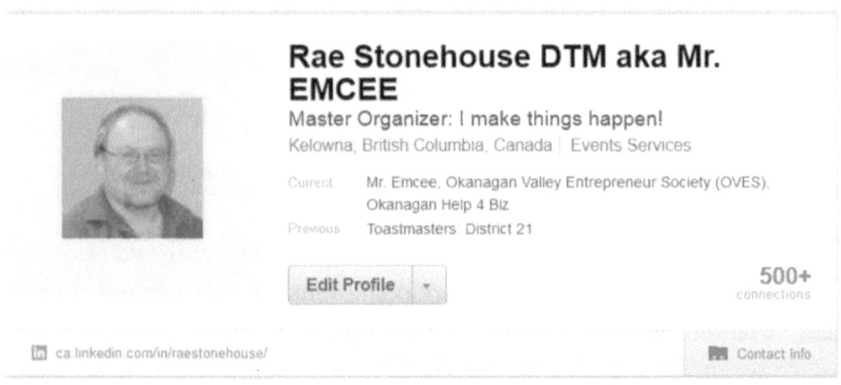

I'll show you an updated version of my Linkedin profile in a few moments as well as some problems experienced with the above headline, specifically my photo.

IN THE *BACKGROUND* HEADING YOU CAN ADD A *SUMMARY* OF YOUR experience and what you currently have to offer.

Under *Experience* you can add any experience you want featured. This is a good place to highlight your strengths and accomplishments. You can add bulleted points in this section, but it should not be all bullet points. Write your summary as if you are speaking conversationally to the person reading it.

It might be helpful to take a look at some other Linkedin user profiles to see how they have completed their profile. Every connection you gain won't necessarily be a business prospect for you. However, as you write your profile, you should do so with the intent a prospect will read it.

This is the place to blow your own horn! Make sure you highlight what you want the reader to see and to remember. Some people take a factual or chronological approach to creating their profile, others more of a promotional or marketing one. My original profile included references to my nursing career and was designed for the possibility of using it for job search purposes. As I am approaching the end of my nursing career and moving into other ventures, I have removed references to my profession in favor of my entrepreneurial ventures and my volunteer life.

Should You Write in the First Person or the Third Person?

This is a contentious question among so-called Linkedin profile creating experts. There doesn't seem to be a best-practices answer to the question and seems to be based on the individual's opinion, rather than hard facts.

Writing in first-person looks like this: "I did this, this and this... then I..."

Proponents of creating your Linkedin content in the first-person argue you should be having a one-to-one discussion with your Linkedin profile reader. Some believe that not writing in the 1st person is a missed opportunity to have a conversation with your reader. After all, they are reading your Linkedin profile for a reason.

From a self-promotional perspective and mine, I believe there is value in writing your copy in the third person. Sure, it may seem weird at first, but it does get easier in time.

Writing in the third person is more likely to seem less like bragging than when done in the first person to the person reading your Bio. Once again, my opinion.

Some believe the first person communication pronoun i.e. 'I' might be proper for:

- a diary entry
- personal testimonial
- dating service post
- autobiography or
- cover letter on an employment application.

Even though you are writing your profile in the third person, everybody knows *you* wrote it. It can be a thin line between self-promotion and bragging. I'm with Walt Whitman, American Cowboy Poet who said "If you done it... it ain't bragging!"

Which ever format you choose, it is important to maintain it throughout your promotional copy. Equally important is to pay extra attention to the tense you are using.

Did you do something in the recent past, or the far past? Are you still do something in the present you want to draw attention to?

Here are some general tips to maximize your Linkedin profile:

- Capitalize properly. "mary smith" is less professional than "Mary Smith."
- Proofread, proofread, proofread.
- Avoid industry jargon as much as possible.
- Avoid acronyms. If you must use them, explain the acronym in the first appearance of it in your profile. Example: ASAP (as soon as possible).
- Use a professional head-shot photo of yourself for your profile. More about that later.

An earlier version of my Linkedin profile (see below) was written tongue-in-cheek. It had the following opening sentences:

<<How many people can honestly say they spent part of their formative years in a maximum-security hospital for the criminally insane?

Rae can! True, he was working as a staff in the Dietary Department and was able to go home every evening at the end of his shift but, that experience has had a lasting effect on him.

Over the past 30+ years Rae has been working as a Registered Nurse, predominantly in the field of mental health/psychiatric nursing.>>

In that version I had taken a promotional approach many would find uncomfortable using. It didn't seem to have held me back any for those who had wanted to connect with me.

Currently I am using a more formalized profile overview focusing on my book writing and publishing, yet still promotional in nature.

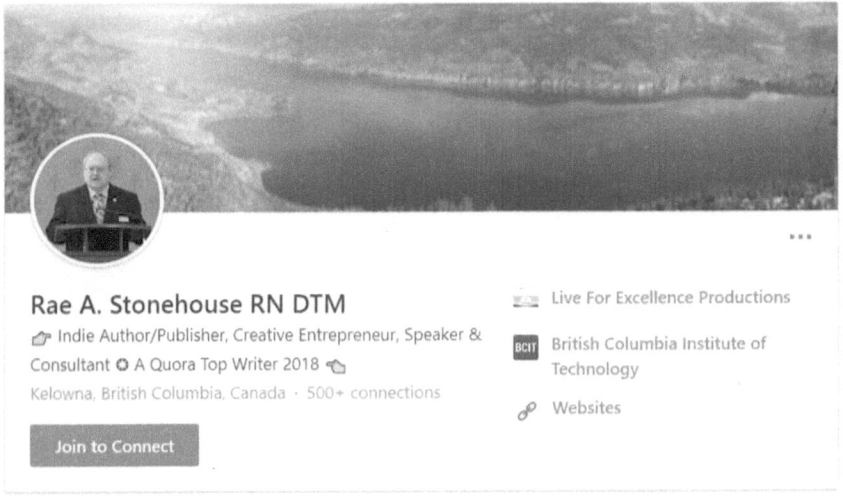

Rae A. Stonehouse is a Canadian born author & speaker.

His professional career as a Registered Nurse working predominantly in psychiatry/mental health, has spanned four decades.

Rae has embraced the principal of CANI (Constant and Never-ending Improvement) as promoted by thought leaders such as Tony Robbins and brings that philosophy to each of his publications and presentations.

Rae has dedicated the latter segment of his journey through life to overcoming his personal inhibitions. As a 25+ year member of Toastmasters International he has systematically built his self-confidence and communicating ability.

He is passionate about sharing his lessons with his readers and listeners. His publications thus far are of the self-help, self-improvement genre and systematically offer valuable sage advice on a specific topic.

His writing style can be described as being conversational. As an author Rae strives to have a one-to-one conversation with each of his readers, very much like having your own personal self-development coach.

Rae is known for having a wry sense of humor that features in his publications.

To learn more about Rae A. Stonehouse, visit the Wonderful World of Rae Stonehouse at https://raestonehouse.com or 250-451-6564

SPECIALTIES:

➤ Author of self-help books & on-line courses

➤ Speech presentation coaching & training

➤ Communicating & leadership skill development

➤ Keynote, workshop, seminar presenting & writing

➤ Facilitating/group moderating

➤ Website development & maintenance (Joomla & Wordpress)

➤ Recognized as a Top Writer 2018 at Quora for over 800 answers & 1 million answer views

A FEW MOMENTS AGO I MENTIONED HAVING A PROFESSIONAL HEAD shot photo featured in your opening profile.

Despite being told not to, people do judge books by their covers and in this case make snap decisions based on an individual's photo.

This is the place to insert a professional-looking head shot photo of yourself, not a picture of your pet, your favorite vehicle or you wearing a bathing suit. Save that for Facebook.

Linkedin has strict rules about photos and you don't want to give them a reason to kick you out.

You only have about two to three seconds to make a good first impression when someone checks out your profile for the possibility of doing business with you. Do you really want to waste the opportunity?

In the previous graphic where I displayed my profile as a Master of Ceremonies at the time, I experienced some problems with my head shot photo.

At the time, I considered myself as a casual type of person. The photo encapsulates me well. I've worn the same style of shirt for decades as well as shorts. I wear shorts year round at home, as I am at this moment writing this. That's who I am.

At the time, I was a member of a breakfast networking club where we helped others get referrals for their business and hopefully gain some in return.

One of my group colleagues approached me to tell me that he and a colleague were looking at my Linkedin profile and his colleague commented he wouldn't hire me as an emcee because my profile picture looked too casual.

He believed if I was marketing myself as a professional emcee, I should look the part in my profile photo.

I agreed with him and promptly updated my photo to a more professional looking one that I use to this day.

The irony of this story was we were at a professional referral marketing breakfast meeting, still in the midst of winter weather and the individual telling me this was wearing a summer golf outfit including brightly colored shorts. I was dressed business casual in a sports jacket and slacks. He definitely was not walking his talk.

Honors & Awards:

Another feature to add to your Profile is *Honors & Awards*. If you have some and they are related to your profession or business venture, this is the place to promote them. I wouldn't recommend listing your first-place bowling trophy unless you happen to be a professional bowler and you wanted people to be aware of the fact.

Publications:

You can promote *publications* you have created and/or published as well as websites you have created or are associated with.

Recommendations:

As you build your network, you can solicit *recommendations* from people you have assisted in some capacity or conducted business with. These are testimonials that can prove to be quite powerful in helping someone who has come upon your name when they have been researching a specific search term in making a decision to contact you or not. You in turn, can provide recommendations for others you have worked with.

As you build your network, it is worthwhile providing testimonials for other Linkedin members you have worked with, assuming you have something positive to say about them of course! The Law of Reciprocity often kicks in when you do so. When you submit a recommendation that has been unsolicited by another, they often feel obligated and create and submit a testimonial on your behalf in return.

Skills & Endorsements is a category Linkedin seems to believe has great value. I believe it would work against you if you didn't have anything in this area however, whether it benefits you in any way, I don't think so. Whereas the *Recommendations* section requires some thought by the contributor, the *Skills & Endorsements* section only requires a click by the endorser.

I've been highly recommended by connections I have never met and am unlikely to meet. Where is the value… or the credibility for that matter of these endorsements?

With a little work, you can create a Linkedin profile that grabs the interest of the reader and has a higher chance of creating an opportunity.

Something to remember is the search engines will not only index and post your Linkedin profile, but it will often link you with everyone that you are linked to. For example, if a person is searching for someone you are linked to and they have used their name as the search criteria, there is a high chance your name will appear in the search results for the other person.

Your chances of being found in the search engines increase even more if you have chosen your keywords in your personal profile carefully.

So why bother doing this much work? A big part of networking is being visible. If people don't know you, they won't likely do business with you. As an event planner working with small business owners and entrepreneurs, I used the Linkedin Search feature frequently to target my search for whatever field or profession I was looking for.

When I am invited by somebody to connect with them in Linkedin the first things I check out is their photo, their profile and the number of people they have connected with.

I tend to be suspicious when I see only a small amount of content posted under their Profile. Either they are just starting to create their profile, they are too lazy to upload content, they really don't buy into the concept of sharing personal info on Linkedin or perhaps they are paranoid and don't want to share anything. It could be any of those reasons but I as the visitor to your site shouldn't have to jump to conclusions as to why you don't have much content posted.

LINKEDIN CAN BE YOUR PERSONAL RESEARCH DEPARTMENT:

Once your profile is posted, you are able to start connecting with other members.

You can also research a person you want to connect to without ever having to leave the comfort of your home. Mobile apps on your smart phone also mean you can research somebody when you are out and about.

The Basic Linkedin package anyone can get for free includes a few features that can aid your research.

You can search for people, jobs, companies by inserting text into the text box and clicking on the Add new search icon graphic.

Linkedin originally had a feature that allowed you to do an Advanced Search. With their moving to a revenue-raising model, sadly this is no longer available for free. You can still access it however, as the saying goes "it'll cost you!"

An additional search technique is to search for the individual through your favorite search engine. Linkedin and Facebook profiles seem to get indexed quite readily. With many people sharing the same name, ensure that you have identified the correct person.

ACTION ITEMS:

1. Develop a descriptive headline statement.
2. Write your content from a self-promotional perspective.
3. Start creating content for each area of your Linkedin profile.

4. Decide whether you will write from a first person or third person perspective.
5. Add a professional head-shot photo of yourself.
6. Create a summary of what you have to offer.
7. Research other Linkedin member's profile to see how they complete their profiles.
8. Add your Honors & Awards.
9. Add your Publications if you have any. Don't forget to add a link.
10. Ask for recommendations from people that you have worked with.
11. Provide recommendations for people that you have worked with.
12. Check your Linkedin profile content for typos.

IN THE NEXT CHAPTER, WE LOOK AT TECHNIQUES TO EXPAND YOUR connections by using Linkedin.

REACH OUT AND LINK SOMEBODY

In this chapter we look at techniques to expand your connections by using Linkedin.

A network is composed of more than one person. If you don't reach out and invite somebody to connect, or you don't receive any invitations to connect, then you don't really have a network.

Sending out an invitation to another Linkedin member can be a challenge for many people, especially if you're shy. We can tend to second guess ourselves... "Why would anyone want to connect with me?"

The Linkedin program will automatically send you notifications of people you might know and ask you whether you would like to connect with them. This can be a double-edged sword as the saying goes.

On one side, if you are connected with somebody, Linkedin will send you a list of names of people they are connected to and ask you if you would like to invite them to connect. If the names presented are people, you already know and they would know you, by all means send them an invitation to connect.

The other edge of the sword comes into play when you submit an invitation to somebody you know and they respond to the invitation with the answer they don't know you.

A few years back, while using the Linkedin app on my Iphone, I was sending out numerous invitations to connect with people who I thought would recognize my name only to find they didn't and Linkedin decided to punish me.

Apparently if too many people say they don't recognize you it triggers something in the system that takes away your privilege to send out an invitation to people you would like to connect with.

At the time, while seemingly being punished for what Linkedin encouraged me to do, they added the extra step of having to add the individual's e-mail address as part of my invitation. This in essence, limited me to only inviting people to connect who I already had their email addresses.

Here is a list of tips to prevent invitation restrictions from the Linkedin site:

- Invite only people you personally know.
- Invite only those you'd recommend to others.
- Personalize your invitation message. Explain how you know them, or why you want to connect.
- Add a current head-shot photo to your profile so people will recognize you.
- Use an *InMail* or *Introduction* if you don't know someone's email address. (these are currently paid features)
- Use the *Ignore* button for invitations from someone you know but choose not to connect with.
- Only use the *I Don't Know* option when you truly don't know the member.

ACTION ITEMS:

1. Send invitations to connect to people that you know and would likely know you.
2. Respond to invitations to connect from people you know.

In the next chapter we look at an assessment form for evaluating your Linkedin profile.

∽

"To position yourself ahead of your competition, you have to negotiate from strength: Who you are, who you are perceived to be, who is on your side." Patricia Fripp

"Some things you have to do every day. Eating seven apples on Saturday night instead of one a day just isn't going to get the job done." Jim Rohn

"You cannot succeed by yourself. It's hard to find a rich hermit." Jim Rohn

LINKEDIN PROFESSIONAL PROFILE ASSESSMENT

Here is a form I created and have been using to assess business professional's Linkedin on-line presence.

NOTE: THIS ASSESSMENT INCLUDES BOTH SUBJECTIVE & objective data.

DATE OF ASSESSMENT:

Name:

Title:

Title SEO optimized? Yes No

Title Search Results 50 km radius:

Professional Headline:

Optimized? Yes No

Current Experience: Prioritized? Yes No

Previous Experience: Relevant? Yes No

Photo: Yes No

Is Photo clear? Yes No

Is Photo professional? Yes No

Is Photo current: Yes No

Is Contact Info Posted: Yes No

Is Contact Info up-to-date? Yes No Don't Know

Are there more than 501 connections? Yes No

Is the Public Profile URL optimized? Yes No

Are there any Posts? Yes No

Are they consistent with profile? Yes No None posted

Background Section

Summary:

Written in resume style? Yes No

Written in promotional Style? Yes No

Value statement/USP (Universal Sales Proposition) included? Yes No

Reader attention grabbed? Yes No

Is Summary written in the 1st person? Yes No

Is Summary written in the 3rd person? Yes No

Is the person consistent throughout copy? Yes No

Is active language used? Yes No

Is passive language used? Yes No

Is correct grammar used? Yes No

Is the tense consistent? Yes No

Are there any unexplained acronyms? Yes No

Does the Summary feature the business Yes No... or the person behind the business?

Yes No Or both?

Are Specialties highlighted and expanded upon? Yes No

Has color been included i.e. graphics? Yes No

Have promotional documents been uploaded? Yes No

Has published work been uploaded? Yes No

Has Slide Share been utilized? Yes No

Experience

Is the Experience section prioritized so that current or most important items display first?

Yes No

Is the copy professionally written? Yes No

Reader attention grabbed? Yes No

Are Experience entries written in the 1st person? Yes No

Are Experience entries written in the 3rd person? Yes No

Is the person consistent throughout copy? Yes No

Is active language used? Yes No

Is passive language used? Yes No

Is correct grammar used? Yes No

Is the tense consistent? Yes No

Are there any unexplained acronyms? Yes No

Has colour been included i.e. graphics? Yes No

Have promotional documents been uploaded? Yes No

Has published work been uploaded? Yes No

Has Slide Share been utilized? Yes No

Has previous or current Volunteer Work been identified? Yes No

HONORS & AWARDS:

Have an Honors & Awards been highlighted? Yes No

If so, is there a good explanation to support it? Yes No

Skills & Endorsements:

Have personal skills been identified? Yes No

Have the Top 10 skills been prioritized? Yes No Don't Know!

Are there any endorsements for the skills identified? Yes No

Publications:

Have any publications been uploaded? Yes No

Do they add to the profile or serve a purpose? Yes No N/A

Education:

Is a school or institution identified? Yes No

Is a specific program or course mentioned? Yes No

Are the years attended identified? Yes No

Additional Info:

Have any interests been identified? Yes No

Have any organizations been identified? Yes No

Have any languages besides English been identified? Yes No

Have any Volunteer Experiences & Causes been identified? Yes No

Are there any recommendations i.e. testimonials? Yes No

If any Groups have been joined, do they add to the profile? Yes No

Are any of these being followed?

News? Yes No

Companies? Yes No

Schools? Yes No

SEARCH ENGINE RESULTS: LISTED?

Google: Yes No

Bing: Yes No

Yahoo: Yes No

UPON COMPLETION OF THE ASSESSMENT I WOULD PROVIDE THE client with a copy of the assessment along with a list of suggestions they might take to improve the effectiveness of their Linkedin profile.

LINKEDIN: BUT WAIT... THERE'S MORE!

I've found there is always more. We have been exploring ways to leverage Linkedin to promote and market yourself.

Here are more suggestions we didn't cover in previous chapters.

Linkedin Groups: At one time the Linkedin Groups feature was an excellent method to expand your network and connect with other Linkedin group members who share your interests. This seems to have gone by the wayside and Groups are no longer effective.

Members don't seem to participate in the groups as they once did, and it seems the number of lurkers far outweigh the regular participants.

You might be better to participate in a Facebook Group related to your interests.

Linkedin Long Articles: Writing and publishing an article on a subject you were experienced in was a good way to attract interest to you and your cause. It is still available, but seems to be out of favor lately. A few years back, whereas I would upload an article of 2000 words or so, I would get a thousand or so views. Lately, I'm likely to get less than one hundred views.

I think what is happening is we are used to the TV style of sound bite, where the information is dished to us in short, choppy segments. Our collective attention spans are getting shorter, and we are not tolerant of reading longer articles. Linkedin Posts seem to be in favor right now.

Linkedin Posts can be as simple as posting a comment of something you are interested in or a cause you want to promote.

Many people curate and share articles they have found from other sources, which in turn helps their name and profile to be seen.

Video is very popular now, and many business professionals are using it for self-promotion. While I have seen some well done and effective ones, I have also seen my share of smarmy ones.

If you write a blog, posting it as a Linkedin Post can help you expand your reach and create a following. Like anything else in social media, the value is in your content being liked and shared. This helps to raise a public awareness of you and perhaps your content.

Action Items:

1. Research Linkedin Groups to see if there are any you are interested in.
2. Start monitoring the Update feature. Post your own updates or comment on others.
3. If you have written a blog or an article on a subject you are interested in, publish it as a post or Article and see how it fares.
4. Create a Powerpoint presentation for the Slideshare application and add to your profile.
5. Search for groups that you are interested in and/or that would allow you to be visible in. Participate in these groups on a regular basis.
6. Create a database of contacts.

In the next chapter we look at even more strategies for promoting yourself on-line via Linkedin.

~

"Believe and act as if it were impossible to fail." Charles F. Kettering

"Success seems to be connected with action. Successful people keep moving. They make mistakes, but they don't quit." Conrad Hilton, 1887-1979, American Hotelier, Businessman, Founder, Hilton Hotels

"The most important single ingredient in the formula of success is knowing how to get along with people." Theodore Roosevelt

BLOW YOUR OWN HORN ON-LINE

In this chapter we look at even more strategies for promoting yourself on-line via Linkedin.

I've mentioned it a few times already in this book. To be successful in business, you need to be able to self-promote... blow your own horn so to speak. The same applies in being a successful networker. If you are researching others, likely they are researching you as well. Make sure you give them something to remember you by.

If you are providing a service or a product that others do as well, you will need to try to stand out from the crowd. Linkedin Basic includes *Slide Share* which allows you to upload a Powerpoint Presentation to www.slideshare.net and have it be accessible on your Profile. It can be a great way to promote yourself and your product or service.

The *newsfeed* section of your profile gives you up-to-date notifications from those you are connected to. Ask a question, share a thought or post an article. This feature can be a good way to send out announcements about special projects you are involved with or to promote something of importance to you. If you have a blog and you have just released the latest edition, promote it here. While it is possible to do, resist the urge to have your Facebook and Twitter account automatically post your content to Linkedin. Each of these three social media venues has their advantages but what works in one might not in the other.

The *newsfeed* is also a great way to keep tabs on the interests of people you may be considering networking with. With each post you have the opportunity to *Like*, *Share* or *Comment*. This can be a good way to start an on-line relationship. It can make it easier for you if and when you actually meet this connection in person. You will already have something in common and can build on it from there.

Sharing your accomplishments will help you find opportunities to teach others, which is part of the process of networking. Be proud of all your accomplishments, whether they seem small, large, significant, easy or difficult. Allow your natural talents & abilities to be the gift you give to your network.

The concept of 'blowing your own horn' may be difficult for some people. Many of us have been taught that talking about yourself is bragging.

As mentioned earlier, I believe it was Walt Whitman who said "If you done it, it ain't bragging!"

A technique that works well at removing the illusion of bragging is to submit an update focusing on someone else. An example could be "I would like to thank XXX for inviting me to speak at their recent conference on my favorite topic of Conflict Resolution!"

If XXX is a member of Linkedin, the message will show up on their Updates as well as yours.

So, on one hand, you are thanking the other person who will likely appreciate being recognized publicly, it will also draw attention to your name and whatever you are trying to draw attention to. In this example, I am focusing on speaking about conflict resolution. This falls into a 'win-win' situation and would increase the likelihood might research the fact I present seminars on conflict resolution.

. . .

Action Items:

1. Research Slide Share to see if it might work for you to display your creative content.
2. Check out your Linkedin Newsfeed for articles of interest and share them to increase your exposure.
3. Decide whether you want to notify your Linkedin connections every time you update your profile or not. You can turn the notification feature off or on in your Linkedin Settings.

In the next section we look at networking as a way to develop your connections and opportunities to build your personal brand and market yourself.

"Don't wait for a ship to come in, swim out to it." Anonymous

"Don't bring your need to the marketplace, bring your skill. If you don't feel well, tell your doctor, but not the marketplace. If you need money, go to the bank, but not the marketplace." Jim Rohn

"The success you are enjoying today is the result of the price you have paid in the past." Brian Tracy

PART II
NETWORKING FOR BUSINESS SUCCESS

NETWORKING FOR BUSINESS SUCCESS

A book about self-promotion and personal branding wouldn't be complete without a discussion on the subject of networking.

In this section we look at networking as a way to develop your connections, build your personal brand and market yourself to create opportunities.

Networking is an acquired skill developed from training, practice and experience.

Networking, whether for pleasure or business, is a perfect opportunity to promote yourself.

In fact, promoting yourself is a *major* part of networking, especially for business.

Many people spend time *networking* but not so much on learning *how* to network.

Only a small percentage of business networkers actually study *how to* network.

To be successful in networking, you need to develop the right mind and skill set.

While you are thinking about becoming a better networker, you need to also think about *why* you are networking in the first place.

Networking opens you up to possibilities.

Expanding your network increases the possibility for referrals to come your way.

Referrals mean potential business.

I'm fond of a quote by John Jantsch, Duct Tape Marketing... "networking isn't something that you do before work or after work. It is work!"

Over the next few chapters, I will be sharing with you some strategies I developed based on my research in writing my book **Power Networking for Shy People: How to Network Like a Pro.**

I have identified three phases to a networking opportunity:

- Pre-Networking Phase
- Live Face to Face Networking Phase
- Post Networking Phase

As we proceed through this section on networking, we will peel back layers of our onion and take an in depth look at each of these phases.

Before we explore the three phases though, let's look at what networking *is* and *isn't*.

Networking is:

- Networking is "do onto others."
- Networking is going the extra mile, taking the next step.
- Networking is an attitude, an approach to life.
- Networking consists of gathering, collecting and distributing information.

- Networking is promoting, empowering, supporting, nurturing, connecting and relating to other people.
- Networking is a communication process, exchanging information & receiving advice & referrals.
- Networking is creating relationships whereby you can help others achieve their goals, which in turn will help you achieve yours.
- Networking is people connecting with people, linking ideas & resources.
- "Networking is communication that creates the linkage between people & clusters of people." John Nesbitt
- Networking is establishing connections that are mutually satisfying, helpful & uplifting.
- Networking is about results & relationships, effectiveness & efficiency, graciousness & persistence.
- Networking is efficient because we use the skills, strengths & expertise of others.
- Networking shouldn't be about selling, it should be about seeking common ground or opportunities.

On the other hand,

Networking isn't:

- Networking is not prospecting.
- Networking is not about getting someone else to say or do what you want.

Networking has been around for ever and always will be.

Networking leads to new relationships, new opportunities & greater accomplishments.

EARLIER IN THIS CHAPTER I MENTIONED A BOOK I HAD WRITTEN about Power Networking.

The book is focused on helping shy people become better networkers but has strategies suitable for all networkers.

Power Networking means the power that comes from a spirit of giving and sharing.

To be *powerful as a networker* you must acknowledge and appreciate the power of networking and your own power as a networker.

As a *power networker*, you should look for opportunities to contribute your ideas.

The buzzword for conducting business effectively in the new millennium may very well prove to be "networking."

In turn, the key element of a networking interaction is the elevator pitch or elevator speech as some would call it.

We'll start with what I have categorized as the *Pre Networking Phase*. These are activities you can do well in advance of attending a live networking event.

Having a well-prepared elevator speech is a basic yet integral self-promotion technique.

We used them as children... "you show me yours and I'll show you mine!"

Well perhaps not quite the same but at its essence it's an opportunity to show your stuff and to learn about the other person.

Assuming they follow the rules of course.

The basic premise is to imagine you are sharing an elevator ride with a person who could be influential in advancing your business or career.

You have the duration of the elevator ride to impress upon this individual why they should buy into your cause or at least agree to talk to you some more about it.

In the next section we explore the *Pre Networking Phase* of business networking. We develop strategies you can do before you meet people face-to-face.

"You don't become enormously successful without encountering and overcoming a number of extremely challenging problems." Mark Victor Hansen

"Success is neither magical nor mysterious. Success is the natural consequence of consistently applying basic fundamentals." Jim Rohn

"Success is nothing more than a few simple disciplines, practiced every day; while failure is simply a few errors in judgment, repeated every day. It is the accumulative weight of our disciplines and our judgments that leads us to either fortune or failure." Jim Rohn

PRE-NETWORKING PHASE

In the next few chapters we explore the *Pre Networking Phase* of business networking. We develop strategies you can do before you meet people face-to-face.

WE START OFF WITH HOW AND WHY TO CREATE AN ELEVATOR PITCH.

CREATING YOUR ELEVATOR PITCH

In this chapter, we explore *how* and *why* to create an elevator pitch.

The buzzword for conducting business effectively in the new millennium may very well prove to be 'networking.' In turn, the key element of a networking interaction is the elevator pitch or elevator speech, as some would call it.

The basic premise is to imagine you are sharing an elevator ride with a person who could be influential in advancing your business or career. You have the duration of the elevator ride to impress upon this individual why they should buy into your cause or at least agree to talk to you some more about it.

You need to develop your elevator pitch like you would a formal presentation.

Just because you are introducing yourself conversationally in a 1 to 1 or a small group doesn't mean that you should wing it.

Preparation is the key to your success.

Follow these steps to develop your unique pitch.

The first thing to keep in mind is to describe yourself as a *solution* to a *problem*.

The most important part of your elevator pitch is your opening sentence. You need to grab your audience's attention by telling what is unique about what you do.

In that very first sentence you need to say your name, your business' name and describe yourself as a solution to the problems your clients, customers or business associates face.

Listeners don't usually care about your job title as much as what you can do for them.

When creating the first line of your elevator pitch, put yourself in the audience's shoes and answer the age-old question "What's in it for me?"

A superior elevator pitch increases your heart rate. It speaks to who you really are and what excites you about your business.

If you don't get excited about it, who will?

In the next section we'll explore the details you need to include in your elevator pitch.

Your pitch needs to address the Five Ws. (Who, What, Why, When & Where)

Your first step is to develop answers to the following questions:

- What does your business do? (For example, begin your answer with "We provide.")
- Whom does your business do it for? (For example, begin your answer with "For small and mid-sized healthcare providers.")
- Why do they care? Or, What's in it for them? (For example, include in your answer "so that they can...," "who can no longer afford...," or "who are tired of...")
- Why is your business different? (For example, begin your answer with "As opposed to..." or "Unlike...")

- What is your business? (For example, begin your answer with "My business is an insurance against...")

Don't forget to include your USP, your hook.

It's a good way to close off your elevator pitch. For example, using my former business... "Mr. Emcee Your Okanagan Event Planner of Choice. From start to finish... we do it all!"

If you are wondering what a USP is, a quick definition it is your *Universal Sales Proposition.* We explore it in greater detail in the next chapter, Developing Your USP.

If you are allowed extra time for your elevator pitch and after you describe the problems you solve, tell a short story to explain your motivation for doing what you do.

This story should be something exciting... "the aha!" moment where you realized you had to do what you do. Or you could tell a story that illustrates how exceptionally good you are at your craft.

Conclude your pitch with an open-ended question to your audience --- one that can't be answered with a simple "yes" or "no" answer.

Closing with a question can draw the listener in, serving as a foundation for a deeper conversation and collaboration and eventually a relationship.

Make sure you prepare, rehearse and regularly revise your elevator pitch to effectively market yourself and capitalize on opportunities that come your way --- whether you are in an elevator or not!

Here are some important considerations to keep in mind:

- Don't confuse people with your pitch.
- No one needs to hear your entire work history on first meeting you.
- No matter how tough it's been, you don't need to tell a sob story, paint a positive picture.
- You need to be congruent with your professional image.

- As the saying goes you need to walk your talk.
- If you are marketing yourself as a wellness coach it would not work for you if you were sick quite often or were carrying 20 to 30 extra pounds.

Here is an easy to follow template for a 30-second elevator pitch:

Start off with your...

Opening Salutation: (Good morning, good afternoon, good evening)

Followed by...

Your Name:

Followed by...

Your Business Name:

Followed by your...

USP: (what is unique about what you do?) (How are you a solution to the problem?)

Followed by...

Closing Comments: (Repeat your name & business name and add a hook)

** For longer time allowances factor in an anecdote and/or close by starting a dialogue.

ACTION ITEMS:

1. If you haven't already, create at least one version of your elevator pitch and preferably more than one. Remember it's a work in progress.
2. Does your elevator pitch address the Five Ws?
3. Practice delivering your elevator pitch out loud.

4. Deliver your elevator pitch at a networking event, either to one individual or to a group.
5. In the next chapter we look at developing your USP. So what's a USP?

∼

"What people get admired and appreciated for in community are their soft skills: their sense of humor and timing, their ability to listen, their courage and honesty, their capacity for empathy." M. Scott Peck

DEVELOPING YOUR USP

In this chapter we look at developing your USP.

So what's a USP?

Your unique selling proposition (a.k.a. *unique selling point, universal selling point or USP*) is a marketing concept used to differentiate yourself from your competitors or others in the marketplace.

The USP is the foundation of a marketing strategy for any business. It forms the foundations for the creation of all marketing collateral: ads, landing pages, content, keywords, audiences, podcasts and more.

Some good recent examples of products with a clear USP are:

- Head & Shoulders "You get rid of dandruff."

Some unique propositions that were pioneers when they were introduced:

- Dominoes Pizza: "You get fresh, hot pizza delivered to your door in 30 minutes or less--or it's free."
- Fed Ex: "When your package absolutely, positively has to get there overnight"
- M&Ms: "Melts in your mouth, not in your hand"
- Metropolitan Life: "Get Met, It Pays"

When advertising, each advertisement must say to the reader: "Buy this product and you will get this specific benefit." The proposition must be one that the competition either cannot or does not offer.

Your proposition must be unique and strong.

The term USP has been largely replaced by the concept of a *Positioning Statement*.

Positioning is determining what place a brand (tangible good or service) should occupy in the consumer's mind in comparison to its competition. A position is often described as the meaningful difference between the brand and its competitors. **Source:** Wikipedia

Your USP must speak to the buyer in the language of the buyer about what matters to the buyer.

ELEMENTS OF A USP:

- Outward focus
- Targets a specific group or niche
- Is easily understood and retained
- Offers an obvious benefit
- Avoids jargon (slang)
- Integrates easily with your marketing materials

WHEN DEVELOPING YOUR USP, CONSIDER THE FOLLOWING factors:

- What are the strengths and weaknesses of your competitors?
- Why do repeat clients and customers like you?
- What makes you better than your competitors?
- If you can answer these questions, you can develop a USP.
- You know what makes your company different and better but you must communicate this to prospects. It takes a little time to develop a USP but there's no cost; the USP is of particular importance for digital marketing.

Step 1: Use your biggest benefits.

Step 2: Be unique.

Step 3: Solve an industry 'pain point' or 'performance gap.'

Step 4: Be specific and offer proof.

Step 5: Condense into one clear and concise sentence.

Step 6: Integrate your USP into all marketing materials.

Step 7: Deliver on your USP's promise.

Taglines:

Closely related to developing your USP is developing a tagline.

A tagline is a slogan which succinctly, memorably, and descriptively sums up a company or product.

A tagline is *not* the same as a USP. Your tagline is usually too short to communicate your entire USP. However, a great tagline quickly summarizes the full USP and communicates the key selling proposition in one or two seconds. A USP can be a few words or it can be a full paragraph.

Taglines are used in advertisements to catch the attention of the viewers. Great taglines should incorporate or touch upon the USP, but there are many taglines that don't.

Taglines could (and probably should) be a short, catchy summary of the USP.

Tips on Constructing Taglines:

- Examine other people's taglines to see what makes them work.
- Be precise in what you are saying. Your tagline must be simple, concise, clear, understandable and convey your marketing message.
- Make sure the words make sense and can be understood by an international audience.
- Have relevant content.
- Be exceptionally easy to read. Have words or phrases that connect with your logo or the visual you are using.
- Use active verbs.
- Have a product name that is easy to read.
- Once you create a tagline to support your marketing message, stick with it.
- Use a dictionary and thesaurus to find words to use.

How a Great Tagline Can Help Your Business:

A great tagline isn't just for large businesses. In fact, it's especially important for smaller unknown businesses.

Why? Because most have little to zero brand awareness... and you won't get prospects excited if they aren't even sure what you do.

I was recently blindsided at a Chamber of Commerce function in my city when we were standing in circle participating in what they call a *power networking* session. We were asked what makes us or our business unique. I didn't recognize it as a USP question and provided an ineffective response. If I had recognized it for what it was i.e. a USP question, I would have responded with my tagline "Mr. Emcee is a full service event organizer. From start to finish... we do it all!"

Your challenge is to develop a USP that on one hand is short and to the point, yet is clear enough it captures the essence of your business and will stick in the mind of whoever you are sharing it with. Having it prepared in advance, believing in it and being able to recite it with a moment's notice will go a long way in reducing your anxiety and fear which are all part of shyness, should you face that challenge.

I would also suggest researching your competitors or others in a similar business that are not necessarily your competitors to see if they have chosen a similar USP as you have. I am aware of two business coaches who chose taglines that had only one word different. That one word totally changed the context of their tagline but it really upset one of the coaches accusing the other of stealing her idea, even though they had been developed independent of each other.

As for my own tagline, I'm currently using **"Tips, Techniques & Solutions for Everyday Challenges."**

Action Items:

1. Research your competitors to learn what their USPs are.
2. Create a USP for your business.
3. Share it with colleagues and ask their opinion. Ask if it makes sense. Ask if it is easy to understand. Ask if it captures the essence of your business.
4. Try using it a few times in networking sessions and see what feedback that you get.
5. Research your competitors to learn what their taglines are.
6. Create a tagline for your business.
7. As suggested with your USP share it with colleagues and ask their opinion. Ask if it makes sense. Ask if it is easy to understand. Ask if it captures the essence of your business.
8. Once you are comfortable with your USP and your tagline,

incorporate it into all of your marketing material i.e. business cards, website, voice mail, e-mail signature file.

IN THE NEXT CHAPTER I CHALLENGE YOU TO DEVELOP MORE THAN one elevator pitch.

∽

"Buried deep within each of us is a spark of greatness, a spark than can be fanned into flames of passion and achievement. That spark is not outside of you it is born deep within you." James A. Ray

"It matters only that you manifest your genius; it doesn't matter when. It's never too late or too early." Mark Victor Hansen

Here is how Walt Disney described his role as mentor after he had stopped drawing: "I think of myself as a little bee. I go from one area of the studio to another and gather pollen and sort of stimulate everybody."

HOW HIGH DOES YOUR ELEVATOR GO?

In this chapter, I challenge you to develop more than one elevator pitch.

How high does your elevator go? 30 seconds, 60 seconds, 10 minutes?

How long should my elevator pitch be? Good question! Answer... it depends. Not much of an answer at first glance, but it really depends on the norms or the culture for the location or venue of the networking session. Presenting your 30-minute curriculum vitae wouldn't likely go over very well in a round-robin style of group introduction where the expectation is 30 seconds, not 30 minutes.

Many referral networking breakfast/luncheon groups based on the BNI (Business Networking International) model, limit their members to 30-second elevator pitches. The more members, the longer the activity takes, but at least it gives everyone an opportunity to speak.

Recently I organized a series of Power Networking Breakfasts. It was speed networking at its best, very much like a speed dating concept. Participants were allowed two minutes and thirty seconds to deliver their pitch. Time limits were rigidly followed with Toastmasters style speech timing lights, green, amber and red and a bell to signal the speaker to stop their pitch, then to move on to the next pitcher. The promotional material advised the participant to come prepared with a two-minute elevator pitch and to be prepared to answer a question or two about their pitch.

It was amazing to find that many of the participants faced challenges in trying to fill the two minutes. They had been programmed to speak and sit down within the restriction of 30 seconds.

I believe one of the challenges many of us face is we have been taught from an early age not to brag about ourselves. When it comes to business, if we don't promote ourselves or our business i.e. blow our own horn, then who will?

We should be passionate about our businesses and be able to talk at length about what we do, why we do it and why you should do business with us. In fact, I would challenge you to be prepared to deliver a 30-minute presentation about yourself and/or your business. Arguably it would likely be one of the slowest elevator rides ever, but if you have ever found yourself stuck in one for an extended time, you will know it could very well happen.

A challenge I have faced with having multiple business ventures, volunteer roles, my professional career & pursuits, I could easily take the full thirty minutes for my 30-second pitch allotment. Which wouldn't leave any room for the others.

If you find yourself in a similar situation, refer back to our analogy of the elevator ride. Many larger high rises have more than one elevator. I would challenge you to create multiple elevator pitches you can use to match with the appropriate venue and situation. A social setting may be a good place to talk about some activities you are involved with and touching upon, but not going heavily into what you do for a living.

At a Toastmasters conference I would likely introduce myself as...

"Good morning everyone, I'm Rae Stonehouse. I'm a Distinguished Toastmaster and have been a member for over twenty-five years. So far! I've served as our District 21 Governor a few years back and continue to serve our leaders in multiple roles. My passion is organizing and creating something from nothing. I'd love to hear how your Toastmasters experience has been. Rae Stonehouse."

I've kept it short and sweet and hopefully have piqued someone's interest so they would want to talk to me some more. I haven't mentioned my profession or my business ventures at all. I would likely fit that into the follow-up conversation as the opportunity arises.

Here's an example of an elevator pitch that wouldn't be such a good idea. Let's say I was in a meeting of the senior managers in my organization. It would probably not be well received if I delivered an introductory pitch, highlighting my experience as a union activist. It would be much better to identify my name, my professional designation, where I work, how long and what I bring to the table.

I'm a firm believer in the adage "If the only tool you have in your toolbox is a hammer, then every problem will be a nail." I believe to be an effective networker you need to have a selection of tools in your metaphorical toolbox. Having a selection of elevator pitches to be able to rely on for any situation is one such tool. Don't throw away that hammer, though. Sometimes a hammer is exactly what is needed!

Action Items:

1. Develop several elevator pitches for your different interests.
2. Develop longer elevator pitches to meet specific opportunities.
3. Develop a 7 to 10 minute presentation to showcase you or your business.

IN THE NEXT CHAPTER WE LOOK AT QUESTIONS YOU COULD, SHOULD and probably shouldn't answer when meeting someone for the first time.

"Everything comes to him who hustles while he waits."
Thomas Edison

"You have to do more than you get paid for because that's where the fortune is." Jim Rohn

"The only competition you will ever have is the competition between your disciplined and undisciplined mind." James A. Ray

IT'S ALL ABOUT YOU

One-to-one conversations are an excellent opportunity to promote yourself.

In this chapter we explore questions you should or could answer, questions you probably shouldn't answer and provide you with tools for your Questions Toolbox.

As we are still within the *Pre-Networking Phase*, the following are more strategies you can do before meeting a potential connection.

Questions you *will* answer:

You should be prepared to answer questions about your business or yourself that are legitimate fact-finding questions. After all, who knows more about you or your business than you do? Some questions that come to mind:

- How long have you been in business?
- Do you work alone or do you have others with you?
- Where did you get the idea for your business?
- Had you worked in the industry before you started your business?

- Has it been successful for you?
- Have you experienced any successes or setbacks that you would like to share with us?

I think you get the idea. I would suggest you brainstorm your own list of possible questions somebody could ask you and then create an answer for each of those questions.

I find one example of a situation that creates anxiety in shy people is when they are caught by surprise with a question they are not prepared or are expecting to answer. If it is your business, you really shouldn't be caught by surprise.

A good example to illustrate this point is the late Robin Williams, the comedian. He always seemed to have a rapid-fire response for any question presented to him or a situation that arose. It would appear he was quick witted in his response and was making them up on the spot, but in reality he was extremely well-prepared.

His impromptu i.e. on the spur-of-the-moment comments were well rehearsed. He had one prepared for almost every situation where he could recall and recite it very quickly. You should do the same when asked questions about yourself or your business. Don't be caught off guard!

Questions you won't answer:

There are rude people out there who will ask questions that are none of their business, yet they will ask anyway. You need to be prepared with an answer that informs them politely that it really isn't any of their business. There are also people that are merely inquisitive and don't realize they are asking a question they shouldn't be.

Once again I would suggest brainstorming a list of questions, you would not want to answer and prepare for them.

A few come to mind:

- How much income did you make last year?
- How much income tax did you pay last year?

- Why did you fire…?

There's a style of question you need to be aware of in case you encounter it, and that is the "no win" question. Its intent is to do you harm in some way. An example would be "Is it true you have stopped beating your wife?" To answer "Yes" would imply you do beat your wife. To answer "No" would be equally as incriminating as it would indicate you are still beating her.

A suggested technique to deflect an awkward or embarrassing question is to reply "I wonder why you would ask a question like that?" It takes the power away from the questioner and causes them to justify their own inappropriate question.

Your Questions Toolbox:

I believe I mentioned earlier the value of having different tools available for you to use at different times. Effective communication skills are an asset.

One of the challenges many shy people have occurs in the small talk phase of an interpersonal interaction. The same can apply in a networking scenario where your colleague has delivered their elevator pitch and you yours. What comes next?

If your conversational partner is a skilled communicator you can go along for the ride, if not, it will likely be up to you to take the lead. "But I'm shy" you say. "I can't do that!"

Shyness is about not having the skills that you need in a social situation and it often leads to fear. If you are prepared in advance and have practiced the skills, you reduce the likelihood you will trigger your anxiety. The intent here is you develop a list of questions that allow you to progress the discussion and learn more about the other individual without seeming you are grilling them with your questions.

Here are some examples of questions that can help progress a conversation. I urge you to develop your own, especially ones that feel comfortable for you to use.

- Tell me about your business?
- How is your year/month/week going so far?
- How did you ever get into this business?
- Did you have any experience in this line of work before you actually opened up your own business?
- Have you ever been to one of these networking events before?
- Do you have any advice that you would share with me about business?
- What are you most proud of with your business?
- How do you see the future of your field or industry?
- How do you foresee the future for your business?

Of course, any of these questions may be on the other's list of questions they have chosen not to answer. You won't know until you ask them and who knows where the conversation takes itself as you learn more. You will need to learn to ask more questions based on the answers you receive and how to interject your own experience on the matter into the discussion. This gets easier with practice.

ACTION ITEMS:

1. Develop a list of questions you *will* answer.
2. Create answers for those questions.
3. Develop a list of questions that you *won't* answer.
4. Prepare a response for questions you *won't* answer.
5. Prepare a list of open-ended questions you can use to advance a conversation.
6. 5. Develop interview questions that you can memorize and use at short notice.

IN THE NEXT CHAPTER WE LOOK AT DEVELOPING YOUR VOICE MAIL message for effectiveness.

Be the change you want to see in the world. Mahatma Gandhi (1869-1948)

"To those who have confidence in themselves, change is a stimulus because they believe one person can make a difference and influence what goes on around them. These people are the doers and the motivators." Buck Rogers

"To change your circumstances, first start thinking differently. Do not passively accept unsatisfactory circumstances, but form a picture in your mind of circumstances as they should be. believe and succeed." Norman Vincent Peale

YOUR VOICE MAIL MESSAGE

In this chapter we look at developing your voice mail message for effectiveness.

Nowadays technology is well within the reach of everyone to help promote themselves on-line.

Two different concepts come to mind here. One being drawn from the field of marketing. You apparently have to touch your customer 7 to 11 times before they will do business with you. Now that doesn't mean you need to physically touch them. That very well may cause you some problems you weren't looking for.

A touch or more precisely a 'touch point' is every time your potential customer is exposed to your name and business. An advertisement in the newspaper they have seen would be considered as one touch point, assuming they saw and read the ad. A second might be they have heard a radio ad you have running. This is how brand recognition works. They need to hear your name over and over again to recognize it.

Having a voice mail message that promotes your business when somebody phones it would be considered a touch point.

Secondly, and we've talked about this elsewhere in this book, is people do make snap decisions on you upon first contact. A poorly created and spoken voice mail message will do you more harm than benefit.

Your message should be courteous and welcoming as well as providing information as to when you will get back to the individual or perhaps alternative contact methods. You could also add your tagline or USP to your message. Have some fun with it!

ACTION ITEMS:

1. Customize your voice mail message.

IN THE NEXT CHAPTER WE DIVE INTO THE LIVE FACE-TO-FACE Networking Phase.

> "You can't build a reputation on what you're going to do." -- Henry Ford

> "Each of us must be committed to maintaining the reputation of all of us. And all of us must be committed to maintaining the reputation of each of us." Jim Rohn

> "You cannot speak that which you do not know. You cannot share that which you do not feel. You cannot translate that which you do not have. And you cannot give that which you do not possess. To give it and to share it, and for it to be effective, you first need to have it. Good communication starts with good preparation." Jim Rohn

LIVE FACE-TO-FACE NETWORKING PHASE

Now we move to the face-to-face phase of networking.

YOUR ELEVATOR HAS ARRIVED: WHAT DO YOU TALK ABOUT?

It's showtime!

Meeting somebody for the first time as in a networking situation can often leave you stuck for words.

Your counterpart delivers their elevator pitch and then as they pause to catch their breath they utter "so what do you do?"

You go on to deliver your well-rehearsed pitch for your business.

But did the two of you really communicate?

Communication is a two-way process.

While the other person is sharing their story, you need to be listening closely to them.

This isn't the time to be practicing your own story in your head.

This is the time to listen.

Imagine there will be a test after your partner delivers their personal story.

Besides trying to figure out what their business is about, you should be listening for statements or beliefs similar to yours.

Perhaps you have had similar experiences as they have described.

Research has shown people like to do business with people similar to themselves.

It is also often said that people will do business with friends before strangers.

So how do you rapidly turn an impromptu exchange of elevator pitches into a "best buddy" scenario?

Well... sometimes it does happen by accident.

You will meet somebody and very rapidly find you hit it off, as the saying goes.

If you are a *Law of Attraction* follower, you would say you are resonating.

You are on the same wave length.

But more often than not it doesn't go that way and can be awkward at best.

The solution lays in *you* taking charge of the conversation.

By charge, I don't mean to take control and dominate it at the other's expense.

I mean to be proactive and direct the conversation in the way you want it to go.

Research has also shown people respond well when you ask them questions about something they have just said... asking them to expand upon a point, perhaps.

The usual questions of *who, how, why, when* and *where* can be used to elicit further info effectively as long as you don't come across as giving them the third degree.

"Where were you on the night of...?

"Can anybody vouch for your whereabouts?" may not be the way to win friends and influence people.

Asking more questions of the person is also a highly recommended traditional sales communication method, i.e. that you use the information you have just gathered to tailor your sales pitch for the individual.

While that may be okay if you are actually in a sales situation, I wouldn't recommend it in first-contact networking encounter.

As I said, *most* people will respond well to probing questions as long as they feel you are eager to learn more from them.

You will know fairly quickly if you are dealing with a paranoid individual.

They are out there.

Once you determine whether you have common interests, don't forget to talk about the possibility of doing business together or helping each other with referrals.

Who knows, you may start off business networking and end up with a new best friend.

COFFEE ANYONE?

For effective business networking I recommend the quality over quantity method of networking.

Some would say that networking is a numbers game, the more people you meet, the higher the chances of your meeting someone who can benefit you.

Take, for example, you are meeting someone for the first time and if the setting and conditions permit, they deliver their elevator pitch and you return with yours.

Then comes the awkward moment, what to say next.

You can either carry on conversing about something of no consequence, "Nice day, eh?" until one of you tires of it or you can explore common interests.

Assuming you have a common interest, I would suggest you take the lead in the conversation in getting the other to expand upon the commonality or something they had previously said.

Many networkers make the mistake of trying to sell their product or themselves at this juncture.

Your goal should be to arrange to meet them at another time, perhaps for coffee, to discuss those common areas further.

Get agreement in principle to meet for coffee.

If your conversational partner doesn't make the offer, you should.

This is assuming of course you see the value in meeting this individual for further exploration of common interests.

You may not see any value and they the same.

Coffee chat isn't mandatory.

EVEN THOUGH MANY OF US ARE ELECTRONICALLY CONNECTED TO our offices by our smart phones and can likely check to see if we are available at a certain date and time to make a coffee date, we likely won't.

When you suggest meeting for coffee, later, if the person is willing to set up a date and time, on the spot, I would go with it.

Location can always be determined later by e-mail.

If they aren't willing to set a time and date, I would refer to their business card and say something to the effect of "can I reach you at this e-mail? I'll contact you next week and see if we can set up a time to get together for a quick coffee."

You could then write a short note on the back of their business card to remind you to contact them, and possibly the best time to do so if you are phoning them.

Unfortunately, for many networkers, this is as far as they go.

They don't do the follow-up.

Life gets busy, there is always one more thing to do with your business and before you know it you have lost the window of opportunity.

There is a strong possibility the individual you were networking with also has a list of people they are following up with and other commitments.

It is far too easy to get left by the wayside if you don't take action to stand out from the others.

If you recognize friends at the networking event, should you stop to speak to them?

While one answer might be "No" you already know them, you should be networking with people that you don't know.

Another, more effective answer, would be, "Yes, certainly!"

"Networking is a lot like gardening."

I'm not sure if anybody famous has said that, so I will take credit for it.

Relationships need to be nurtured.

We all have business colleagues or business friends that while we don't necessarily do business with them, we see them regularly at business networking sessions.

"Catching up" is a good way to learn more about the business environment from a different perspective than your own.

It's also a great way to put the word out on what you require for your business or what you have to offer someone else to advance theirs.

People will do business with those they know and care about before they will with someone they don't.

Like watering and fertilizing your garden, business relationships need to be nurtured.

I wouldn't suggest spending too much time with them though as doing so would prevent either of you from the networking for new contacts you likely attended the event for.

This would be another opportunity to set a coffee date if you want to chat at greater length or depth.

Leveraging your colleague's connections can be an effective networking technique.

By asking "Is there anyone here you know and could introduce me to who could help me with...?"

And if there is, have them seek out the referral and make the introduction.

If you are shy and reluctant to meet people for the first time, having a colleague or friend walk with you to make the first contact can take pressure off you.

Action Items:

1. Invite a connection out for a coffee chat for the purpose of getting to know them better and looking for common interests.
2. Do any potential opportunities arise from your coffee chat?

IN THE NEXT CHAPTER WE LOOK AT THE PRACTICE OF PASSING business cards to new connections. Is it outdated or still in practice? We shall see...

BUSINESS CARD CARE, CUSTODY & ETIQUETTE

In this chapter we look at the practice of passing business cards to new connections.

THERE ARE THOSE WHO WILL ARGUE BUSINESS CARDS ARE NO LONGER relevant in today's business networking. I believe they are and if you are planning on doing some serious networking you should have business cards available to present.

Not having a card may be a missed opportunity for you. Besides serving as an introduction for you and your business, they will serve as a visual prompt to remind the other person they met and spoke to you.

Business cards are quite inexpensive to print nowadays, so cost shouldn't be a deterrent to having some printed. If you are in transition and expect your info to change soon, your printer will likely accommodate small batch runs.

Even if you are technically not in business, perhaps in transition and looking for employment, you should still have a card outlining who you are and what you do or the kind of work you are looking for and how someone can get in contact with you.

There are those business people who believe in having their photo as part of the card. Supposedly, I'm guessing here, so you remember them better. It can be problematic if they have used a more youthful picture from yesteryear. We joke about some realtor's (real estate agents) business cards and newspaper advertisements we see locally. Their public marketing image is a young youthful person and when you meet them they are somewhat prune looking i.e. dried up and aged! I feel that I have been tricked. Vanity can affect people in different ways, I suppose.

The Japanese take the presentation of a business card in a one to one networking situation far more serious than we do. To them, ritual is involved. When presented with a business card you are expected to accept it with both hands, hold it in front of you and read the content of the card, both sides. You would then hold it with respect as the other person shares their elevator pitch. You would only place it in your pocket after you had left the person and you would never deface the card by writing on it.

In North America we are a little less respectful. Sometimes, quite a bit! I have met a fellow who within the first seconds of meeting him he announces, "Well let's get this out of the way" and hands me his card. I expect that he wasn't as comfortable or skilled at networking as he thought he was.

I have also seen an influential woman walk up to a group of people and start passing out her business cards. "Here you go, one for you and one for you!" She then left the group and went over to another and repeated the process. It was like she was feeding chickens or passing out candy to children who were trick or treating at her door. The purpose of passing out her business card seemed to be missed. I wonder if she was actually shy and was covering up her uncomfortableness?

So what is the correct way to present your card to another? How and when?

I'm sure everybody has their own view on the matter.

When I have been offered another's business card as part of an introduction that is under way, I will adopt what I described earlier as the Japanese method. I will accept it, quickly read the details and I will keep it in my hand in full view. I see the offering of a business card from another as the cue to offer mine in return. I often make a comment about a detail or an aspect of their business card to reinforce that I have taken a serious look at it.

If I don't see any action from my partner towards offering their business card, I will initiate it myself. Asking, "Do you have a business card?" can be easier than saying "Here is my business card." Of course, their providing a card opens it up for me to provide mine.

I will also listen for a verbal cue of "I should get in contact with you", "I will keep in touch" or anything close to that as a signal for me to offer my card.

In an earlier section, I mentioned the value of having different elevator pitches available for a given situation. At a business networking event, I am prepared to give business cards as the discussion develops. After getting my own cards mixed up far too many times with the cards I have received, I have developed my own system of organization.

I usually wear a blazer with hip pockets. In my left pocket I would have a supply of my business cards. In my right pocket I have a card representing my role as the Chairman of the Board of our local entrepreneurs society. In my wallet, I will carry some cards that I can pass out related to Toastmasters.

When I receive a *new* business card, after reading it, I will insert it into my shirt pocket. As I have several blazers or suit coats, I organize them all the same way. We will talk about name badges elsewhere, but I carry one in each blazer so that it will be there when I need it. If I'm expecting to pass out more than the average amount of business cards at an event I will have an extra supply in my briefcase or my vehicle should I require them.

A female reader of the last paragraph pointed out to me "What if you are wearing a little black dress and carrying a clutch purse where do you put the cards that you have collected?" Having never worn a "little black dress" I can only assume they don't include deep pockets. Perhaps wearing the dress in the first place to a business networking event might be the point to focus on. I make no proclamation of being an expert on women's fashion!

I will even muddy the water a little and ask "Should you give your business card in all situations?"

I've been in interactions where the other individual doesn't seem overly interested in me, or are overly interested in themselves. I may make a judgement call on the spot and choose not to share my business card.

Then there are those who choose not to share business cards. This could be a simple matter of not having cards printed yet or having problems deciding what to put on the card. Not everybody is creative.

I've heard of one woman who when asked for her business card replies, "Oh, I don't do business cards. I prefer to write down the person's name and contact information on my little pad. It's much more personal."

It may be more personal to her, but in today's fast-paced world, this could be an irritant or an imposition to some networkers.

I'm reminded of a young fellow who attended one of my speed networking events I mentioned earlier. He was a salesman for a high-end office furniture business. When I asked him why he didn't have any business cards he replied, "How could anybody forget this smiling face?"

Well, apparently they did. The next time I saw him he was behind the counter of our local Dairy Queen filling ice cream cones.

While it is important to pass out your business card with your accompanying elevator pitch, it is equally important to collect other's business cards.

But what do you do with them when you get them?

Do you throw them into your desk drawer or the corner of your desk to collect dust?

No, that would be a waste of an opportunity.

To be able to build your network of connections who you know and hopefully know you, you need to work with these business cards.

A first step would be to contact all the individuals that you spoke to and received their cards, by sending an invitation to join your network on Linkedin.

It's probably be a good idea by saying that it was good meeting them and reminding them where you met them.

Another idea would be to add their contact info to your Outlook, G-Mail or whatever program you are using.

If you have a regular e-news letter, you could add them to your membership list.

Be sure to provide them an opt out option to keep you out of trouble with the Spam Police.

Action Items:

1. Create and purchase business cards to promote yourself.
2. Develop your skills in receiving and presenting business cards.

In the next chapter we discuss dressing for success. Yes, first impressions do count.

"Organizing yourself is like eating candy, it makes you think twice about doing it... but once you do... the outcome is SWEET!" Doug Firebaugh

"Become a strategic thinker. Set goals for what you want and create organized plans of action to achieve them." Brian Tracy

"Take complete control of your career path by research, planning, and active career development strategies." Brian Tracy

DRESS FOR SUCCESS

I n this chapter, we discuss dressing for success.

MOST OF US HAVE LIKELY BEEN TOLD FROM A VERY EARLY AGE "YOU shouldn't judge a book by its cover." Yet we do it every day, often in the first few seconds of having met someone. We automatically determine whether they are a danger to us, whether we would want to have a conversation with them, whether we would want them as a mate... or to mate with. We do it automatically.

It's part of being human, and our judgement is often made with the clothing the person is wearing as one of our decision-making criteria.

Being dressed *wrong* for a given situation can set you apart so that people do not want to approach you to converse. Remember, as a shy person, having somebody come up to you to talk can be a lot easier than having to make the approach yourself. So don't reduce your chances by dressing wrong.

WRONG? WHAT DOES THAT MEAN? THERE IS A LOT OF ROOM FOR interpretation. What is wrong for one person may be right for another. Many people like to express themselves through colorful clothing or cutting edge fashion. Others don't have a clue when it comes to dressing for the occasion. I attended a black-tie gala awards event. I was in a tuxedo, as was my colleague. We observed some men in their cleanest blue jeans with a black string tie. I think they missed the point.

MY SUGGESTION WOULD BE IF YOU WERE ATTENDING A BUSINESS networking event, then 'business casual' would be appropriate. This can become even more casual in hot climates. If everyone is wearing shorts and you are in your tuxedo, you may get attention, but perhaps not the kind you wanted.

AS FOR DRESSING FOR SUCCESS, IT HAS BEEN PROVEN OVER AND OVER that most people feel better about themselves when they are dressed up.

Dressing for success doesn't have to be expensive. My wife has been quite successful in finding good quality clothing at local thrift shops.

I know one young fellow who tells me he has created most of his business casual wardrobe from also shopping at local thrift shops.

He finds and buys sports jackets that still have a lot of life in them. He then takes them to a seamstress and inexpensively gets them altered to fit him better.

You need every advantage you can get when you are out there networking, marketing yourself. Don't shut the door in your face before it is even opened.

People do judge others by their clothing, don't let them judge you without talking to you first.

What's shaking? In the next chapter we find out.

Action Items:

1. Determine what 'business casual' is.
2. Identify the dress code for business networking events in your community.
3. Assess your personal wardrobe for items you can mix and match.
4. When at a business networking function, assess the clothing others are wearing. Does it work? Does it help them look professional or take away from the effect?

What's shaking? In the next chapter, we find out.

"Dress for success. Image is very important. People judge you by the way you look on the outside." Brian Tracy

"You don't become enormously successful without encountering and overcoming a number of extremely challenging problems." Mark Victor Hansen

"Use the Trial and Success method; learn how to improve and succeed by falling and learning from your mistakes." Brian Tracy

WHOLE LOTTA SHAKING GOING ON

A handshake is more than just a greeting. It is also a message about your personality and confidence level. In business, a handshake is an important tool in making the right first impression.

Before extending your hand, introduce yourself. Extending your hand should be part of an introduction, not a replacement for using your voice.

This isn't the cue to start reciting your elevator pitch though. Extending your hand without saying anything may make you appear nervous or overly aggressive.

On one hand (pun intended!) it would seem shaking someone's hand should be an easy process. We have likely been doing it most of our adult life. On the other hand, some people seem to have problems with it.

I believe part of the problem that creates anxiety is we over think things sometimes. We are anxious because we give more importance to the activity than it really deserves, and it takes on a life of its own... creating anxiety. A self-fulfilling prophecy if there ever was one.

Another part that likely creates anxiety is we can only control our portion of the interaction. If our partner is an experienced hand-shaker, then all should go smoothly, but many aren't.

There are a few different hand-shaking styles that come up in the literature, and I am sure you have likely experienced them yourselves.

I personally don't like grasping someone's hand who has the so-called **"wet fish"** handshake. It can leave you with an obsessive urge to wipe your hand as soon as you can, but fight the urge.

Even worse, there are times my hand is sweating and I don't want the label. I have developed the habit of giving my hand a quick, unobtrusive wipe on my pant leg before offering my hand.

Then there is **"bone-crusher Bill."** The offered hand often comes in as a curve from the hip of Bill with the express purpose of crushing walnuts. Or so it would seem. Bill never seems to realize the pain he causes in others, or the fact people start to avoid him. Word can get around!

Another ineffective handshake I call the **"royal"** handshake. Someone only offers you the tips of their fingers and no matter how you try, you can't seem to grasp more than a few fingers. You are left feeling you were robbed.

The bottom line is to avoid being any of these profiles. If you need to practice at home before going to a networking session, do so.

It seems to becoming more common that friends are hugging when meeting in a social setting. There are many people I call the "huggy" people. I would suggest waiting to see if you offered one rather than expecting one. It could make for an awkward situation if you were to offer a hug on a first contact and it was declined.

Author's Note: At the time of writing this chapter, March 2020, the world has gone crazy with fears of the Coronavirus (COVID-19).

Many public gatherings have been canceled. People have been

changing the way they greet each other. Instead of shaking hands, they are doing fist and elbow bumps.

It will be interesting to see if this world-wide crisis will have a lasting effect on how people greet each other, or if it will just be a knee-jerk response and go by the wayside when it is over.

In the next chapter we look at your personal promotion billboard... your name tag.

~

"Every great success is an accumulation of thousands of ordinary efforts that no one sees or appreciates." Brian Tracy

"Don't wish it was easier, wish you were better. Don't wish for less problems, wish for more skills. Don't wish for less challenges, wish for more wisdom." Jim Rohn

WEAR A NAME TAG

In this chapter we look at your personal promotion billboard... your name tag.

Many networking events you attend will provide a sticky-backed name tag with something like "Hello, my name is..." If the organizers are insistent you wear it, I would suggest you write your name as interestingly as you can, something that will attract another to focus on it.

My preference would be to wear a name badge that professionally displays your name and your business/organization. I believe people tend to scan your name badge when they are first approaching you to see if there is an immediate connection between you and them.

They can also look at it while they are speaking to you to keep your name in their mind. It can help as a reminder to you if you get to the point where you are so overwhelmed with other's names and the networking process that you can look down and remind yourself what yours is.

Here are a couple badges I had made for my wife and I for my business. I purchased two for myself so I could keep one in each of my sports jackets. I was surprised at how inexpensive they were to purchase i.e. $45.00 for three badges.

IN THIS CASE, THE TERM MASTER ORGANIZER, SETS SOMEBODY UP for the inevitable question of "So what do you organize?"

In the next chapter we move into the Post Networking Phase, that is what do we do after we have connected? Hint... follow-up!

"DESIRE IS THE KEY TO MOTIVATION, BUT IT'S THE determination and commitment to an unrelenting pursuit of your goal - a commitment to excellence - that will enable you to attain the success you seek." Mario Andretti

"You've got to get up every morning with determination if you're going to go to bed with satisfaction." George Horace Lorimer

TYPES OF INTRODUCTIONS

In this chapter we're going to focus on different types of situations you may encounter, that will allow you to promote yourself, when you are required to introduce yourself to a group.

These may or may not be good opportunities to use your elevator pitch.

We've talked previously about developing different lengths for your elevator pitch.

And we've talked about having different versions of your elevator pitch to promote whatever aspect of you or your business that you want to highlight.

My local Chamber of Commerce has initiated what they call a *power networking* opportunity and they liken it to speed dating.

The format is that a certain amount of the early bird attendees at their business after hours form a large circle.

Somebody from the Chamber Administration serves as the facilitator and goes around the room having everybody deliver a 30-second pitch.

I've participated in a few of them and have noticed the same people being ineffective in their delivery or squirming because they are uncomfortable with public speaking.

I have also seen some who seem to think that 30 seconds is the same as ten minutes and go on and on. Either they don't clue in or they think that rules are for other people, I say as I stand on my soapbox.

My approach to this scenario is to deliver my 30-second elevator pitch and try to stand out from the others so I will entice them to come up and talk to me after the activity is over.

Another group activity I have participated through my local Chamber of Commerce, is where they count off people in groups of three.

The three people would go off in a separate area of the meeting room.

Each of the three would deliver their elevator pitch to the other two. This would then lead to a discussion among the three looking for common areas of interest.

It does a good job of helping you to meet two new people, but you lose out on hearing people's names and businesses as you would in the larger circle group introductions.

One technique I use is I always start off with a salutation. Example: "Good morning everyone" or "good evening everyone", depending on the time of day of course.

I believe it demonstrates I am confident in what I am saying next.

Another tip I have learned is in how I announce my name in a group setting.

Going around a group and having to announce your name to the group can be stressful for some people

Many people are focused on what they are going to say.

And then they find it difficult to remember the other person's name, let alone their own.

Try saying your first name, followed by a pause then your first and second name.

Example: "Good morning everyone. I'm Rae... Rae Stonehouse..." Try it a few times to see how it feels.

Don't forget to use your name though and not mine.

Another common scenario I have seen used is an icebreaker activity to start off a smaller group activity.

You are asked to interview the person sitting beside you and introduce them to the group.

In essence, you are delivering their elevator pitch for them.

The challenge is there never seems to be enough time for the exercise.

Not only do you have to collect your partner's information, you also have to make sure you have delivered your pitch and verified they've actually heard you.

I would recommend using pen and paper to jot down some notes about your partner.

This will help you keep track of the details you want to share.

I try to keep my notes simple by capturing their name (it is surprising to see how many people actually stumble over this part), the name of their business and an interesting point or two about the individual.

This can be a good time to play detective, using the old standby questions of 'who, why, what, when, where and how.'

It's not a time to use the old pickup line of 'What's a nice guy or girl, like you doing in a place like this?'

But then again, it might just serve to break the ice so that you can gather the information quickly.

It can be an awkward situation for all involved. When delivering my introduction of my partner I always use the same format.

"Good morning/evening everyone. It gives me great pleasure to introduce the lady/gentleman seated to my right/left. They operate a business called... And they provide... Please welcome..."

I often receive favorable comments on these introductions, and it demonstrates my confidence and poise.

However, when my partner introduces me, I really don't have any control of it all and hope they don't butcher it.

I believe the introduction I give can help mitigate any damage my partner does in their introduction of me.

Action Items:

1. Practice interviewing another person and introducing them out loud. If you don't have anyone to introduce, feel free to make up an imagined person i.e. identity & business info.
2. In the next chapter we look at a way to assess your networking effectiveness.

POST NETWORKING PHASE

This chapter carries on with the 3rd phase of networking, the Post Networking Phase I outlined in my book **Power Networking for Shy People: How to Network Like a Pro**.

What's Next?

You've had a good chat with someone at a networking event and you feel there's a chance of possibilities developing.

You part and go your separate ways.

Now what?

Some books on networking I have read would say you should plan your "attack" in advance.

Attack would seem to be a little strong of a word.

Approach might be better.

THE FIRST ACTIVITY IN THE POST NETWORKING PHASE IS *FOLLOWING up:*

Follow-up is Everything! Set up and confirm the coffee meeting.

It can be a great feeling when coming home from a networking event and looking at the stack of business cards you have collected.

You even spoke at length to many of the card-donators.

Some, it can be a little difficult to recall who they were.

"Now was he the tall fellow with the bad hair piece... or was he...?"

You've probably experienced that scenario more than once.

And you know what... perhaps some of the business-people you gave your precious business card to are thinking something similar.

Hopefully not about your bad hair though.

A while back, when I was a member of the Okanagan Business Referral Group, we discussed the issue of follow up.

A member named Mike, related that in his experience, if you follow-up with a lead, it puts you way ahead of those that don't.

He makes a practice of following up with a networking connection within three days of the original meeting and says it is amazing how many people have said "You know, you are one of the few who actually follows up."

Yes, following up can help you stand out from the competition.

The coffee get-together is the opportunity for each of you to share your business details and determine if there is enough reason to continue at another time to develop your relationship further and ideally to do business together.

You might ask "I've contacted them three times by e-mail and even left a couple voice mails but they haven't gotten back to me. What do I do next?"

There could be a legitimate reason for them not getting back to you.

Life happens!

But they could be acting non-assertively and are actively avoiding you.

I would have to respond with "If that was true, is this someone you really want to network with or to do business with?"

If you are to continue, it could easily label you as a stalker.

One suggestion may be to add them to your tickler file.

A couple weeks down the road, ignoring the fact they haven't acknowledged you yet, you would be justified in sending them a message something like "I just noticed we didn't get together a few weeks ago like we said we would.

Where did the time go?

It seems to be picking up speed.

Last time we met we were discussing our common interests of…

Are you still interested in getting together?"

If you still don't receive a response, I would put them in the "inactive" file.

When it comes to networking, to stand out from your competition, remember to follow-up.

Knowledge Is Power! - Research The Person On Google & Linkedin

You can easily research a person on-line who you have set up a coffee appointment with. It should be easy to insert their name into Google, or your favorite search engine Search box and see what comes up. You are not likely to find the nitty gritty on somebody if that's what you are expecting to find, but you will likely find information that can be helpful in learning what their interests and background is.

I have found this to be a helpful strategy in several instances. In one case, an individual had been recommended to me as a possible speaker for a panel discussion I was moderating on the topic of bartering.

My research revealed the individual had several past charges for fraud

BLOW YOUR OWN HORN!

and several more outstanding ones. I saved embarrassing myself by spending a few moments on-line researching.

If you haven't already Google your own name to see what comes up. Sometimes there are some surprises out there that you may not want to be publicly known, yet it is.

ACTION ITEMS:

1. Follow-up with the person you made contact with to set-up a coffee meeting.
2. Research your coffee meeting partner on Linkedin.
3. Google their name to see what arises.
4. Google your own name.

IN THE NEXT CHAPTER WE LOOK AT MAXIMIZING YOUR COFFEE CHAT meeting.

IT'S COFFEE TIME!

In this chapter we look at maximizing your coffee chat meeting.

Coffee chat or meeting somebody for a quick coffee to either meet someone for the first time or to catch up with an old colleague or friend is becoming increasingly popular.

In my city it can be challenging to locate a coffee shop that has room to accommodate a couple people as they are so busy.

SHOW UP A FEW MINUTES EARLY.

Many people experience anxiety over having to show up on time for appointments.

They fret about the possibility of being late.

If you happen to be one, I would suggest arriving a few minutes early.

This would likely mean leaving from your current location in a timely manner.

Ensure you have the correct address of the place you are meeting.

I have been caught more than a few times with showing up at the Starbucks I knew, only to find out there was another new one a way down the road.

I had to hustle to get there.

Getting there early also allows you to choose a good seat.

If you were an undercover operative, i.e. secret agent, you would also have your back to the wall so that you can see who is coming in as well as having a clear escape route planned.

If you're not a spy... well, then never mind!

Rule of thumb...

Whoever makes the invitation for coffee pays.

But don't count on it!

I would suggest you make sure to have enough cash on you or access to debit/credit, so you don't get surprised.

You wouldn't want to work off a cup of coffee by having to work in the kitchen washing dishes.

Don't sell... learn!

This is your opportunity to learn more about the other person as well as to share your ideas.

To learn, you need to ask questions.

Be wary of what I call the bait and switch coffee chat.

It starts off with your coffee partner asking about you, what your interests are and seemingly hanging on your every word.

They ask you what your aspirations are and what you would like out of life.

Then it's their turn to share.

Well, guess what?

They just happen to have the perfect solution for you. A get rich quick network marketing independent associate position and they jump into a full-fledged multi-media presentation right there in the coffee shop.

I'm not saying there is anything wrong about network marketing. I believe in it.

However, I do not believe in being a captive audience to a sales presentation without having the opportunity to say yay or nay.

Look for common areas of interest

The intent of this coffee meeting is to explore if there are common areas between the two of you to build a more in-depth relationship.

If you have researched your coffee partner, this would be the time to fit these tidbits into conversation.

Don't be surprised if they say something to the effect of "You checked me out?" My answer would be "Of course! I check everybody out."

So how long should a coffee chat last?

I've had many of them over the years.

I find that 60 minutes is enough to determine if you have anything in common with the other person and whether there is enough interest to schedule another meeting.

An hour and a quarter can give you some extra time to get to know each other, but I find the conversation tends to drag a little near the end.

So, how can you help the other person?

BNI (Business Networking International) has an interesting catch phrase of "Givers Gain!"

Develop a servant mindset.

What exactly does that mean?

I am not suggesting your role is to wait hand and foot on the other person.

Rather, a servant mindset is one where you offer your services and expertise to the other without the expectation of obligation that they in turn will provide you something.

Nor am I suggesting you work for free or provide free services to them.

I am suggesting you offer your expertise or perhaps access to your connections as a way of promoting their business.

If you are a Law of Attraction believer there is also a Law of Reciprocity.

Loosely described it could be "What goes around... comes around."

Looking at it from a positive perspective, if you provide an act of kindness, there is a high chance it will be returned.

I have experienced some good returns on creating and submitting testimonials to Linkedin for business colleagues.

In the next chapter we discuss an alternative way to developing connections without having to attend large get-togethers.

AN ALTERNATIVE TO ATTENDING LARGE NETWORKING EVENTS

In this chapter we discuss an alternative way to developing connections without having to attend large get-togethers.

I've often heard it said in reference to "self-help," books... "If you get only one gem or a useful tip from a book it makes all of your reading time worthwhile."

While that may be true, it can have you spending a lot of time with your nose in a book.

The same principal can be applied... inefficiently, to your networking activities. "One good contact can make a world of difference in your business..."

In essence you are leaving your success to serendipity.

Serendipity, or leaving everything to chance, while awe-inspiring when it works, is not something you can control or count on.

Does the following scenario sound familiar?

You attend a large event touted as the best networking event in town.

You meet a dozen or so "new" people, new to you that is, not new to everyone else, or so it would seem.

You deliver your 30-second or longer elevator pitch over the ever-increasing din in the packed room.

You go home with a handful of business cards.

The next day or so you face the challenge of contacting all your warm leads.

If this is an activity you aren't fond of, your 200-pound phone handset can be quite daunting. "Hi, this is Rae. We met the other night at..."

"Who?"

Okay, perhaps I'm injecting my own inadequacies here, but I really have heard people agree.

Here is a *power networking technique* to maximize your effectiveness.

If your main purpose in attending a networking event is to get a handful of business cards, then go for it!

An alternative option would be to meet a business colleague or friend you are comfortable with, in a setting conducive to conducting business and compare personal networks.

"I'll show you mine... if you show me yours," so to speak.

For those that are old enough to recall trading baseball or hockey player cards, this isn't what I am suggesting.

A planned approach is best.

For example, if I was looking for a bookkeeper/accountant to take on a volunteer role in a society that I led.

I would meet with somebody who I know has a background in finances and I could specifically ask them who they would know in their network who might meet my search parameters.

At this preliminary stage, it's a matter of brainstorming contact's names.

Write them down on a piece of paper.

This isn't the time to be evaluating each name as to whether they might be interested in participating. Your only task at this point is to generate a list of names.

The idea is to leverage your colleague's network.

With social media being so prevalent nowadays, many of us are well connected.

Well-connected doesn't mean we actually know or have even met the contact though, more of an e-contact if you will.

It probably wouldn't be much of a surprise to find you already know some names generated and they are part of your network.

Our next step is to rate each of the names we have generated as to how well your colleague knows the individual.

Would the individual be surprised if you contacted them saying they were referred by your colleague?

Or would your contacting the individual trigger a "Who?" response.

Generating a list of names isn't of much use unless you get their accompanying contact info.

Now is the time to leverage your connections and make that net work.

Make those phone calls.

Don't forget to spend some time helping your colleague with their networking measures. While it can be said "It's not who you know... it's who knows you!", perhaps we need to amend it to "It's not who you know, it's who knows you know who you know!"

In the next chapter we discuss characteristics of successful networkers and types of networkers.

CHARACTERISTICS OF SUCCESSFUL NETWORKERS

In this chapter we discuss *characteristics* of successful networkers and *types* of networkers.

BNI PROMOTES ITSELF AS BEING THE LARGEST BUSINESS NETWORK IN the world and is founded by Dr. Ivan Misner.

I'm not a BNI member, nor have I ever been one.

I'm impressed by the quality and depth of their effective networking advice.

Here are the **Top Characteristics of Successful Networkers** derived from BNI.

- Having a *giving* philosophy... givers gain.
- Having a *positive* attitude. People hate to do business with grumpy people.
- Network with people that you know. Be a *connector*.

- *Surround* yourself with people *different* from you. They broaden your connections. *Factor* in different races and culture for diversity.

Types of Networkers:

In one of their podcasts Dr. Misner, founder of BNI, identified five types of networkers. Here they are (derived from BNI) that you are likely to meet at a networking function.

I want to discuss them at this juncture because it is easy to make generalizations in life. One generalization being that everyone else is like we are.

It simply isn't true!

As you encounter people in your networking activities, I would suggest you place them into one of the following categories. You may even come up with your own categories.

Why would we want to, you might ask?

It can be helpful to understand where somebody is coming from to determine where they are going.

Let's start off with the first one...

Hermit: Hermits don't have a network, nor do they know how to.

They tend to be "*systems*" oriented, not a "*people*" person.

They avoid networking because they don't how to or they are extremely uncomfortable in doing so.

They can become more comfortable with training.

Hunter: Hunters are looking for quick sales.

They want to "eat what they kill."

They are not into developing relationships.

They are involved in direct sales vs relationship sales.

They are not into nurturing a relationship for future sales.

I tend to call these *sharks* as they seem to use hit-and-run as their networking technique.

You are only of interest to them until they have made the sale and they move on to the next prey... I mean customer.

Schmoozer: This group is easy to recognize.

They seem to have the gift of gab.

Socializing and conversing comes easy to them.

They really enjoy meeting people.

They are often not very good at getting to the next step of developing and nurturing an ongoing relationship.

It is far easier to move on to the next exciting conversation.

Apprentice: I would expect many of us reading this section would fall into the category of Apprentice.

That means that we realize our networking skills are in need of improving, and we accept the fact they will only improve by practicing them.

We are open to making mistakes and learning from them.

Master: The Master Networker is what I would imagine we all aspire to be.

We would like to have all skills come second nature to us and be ready, willing and able to take advantage of opportunities as they come our way.

. . .

IN THE NEXT CHAPTER WE EXPLORE DIFFERENT TYPES OF SITUATIONS you may be required to introduce yourself or others.

"You can't think your way into acting positively, but you can act your way into thinking positively." Nido Qubein

"Act the way you'd like to be and soon you'll be the way you act." George W. Crane

ASSESSING YOUR NETWORKING EFFECTIVENESS

In this chapter we look at a way to assess your networking effectiveness. The content for this chapter is excerpted from my book **Power Networking for Shy People: How to Network Like a Pro**.

I would suggest developing some benchmark performance standards so you can compare each new meeting or interaction. You would conduct this exercise later on after the event was finished.

Some answers lead to yes or no answers. Others may be better answered on a sliding scale. If you keep records of your results, you are better able to track your progress.

Some examples might be:

- I approached someone I didn't know and made the first comment. Yes No
- I listened intently while the other person delivered their elevator pitch before starting mine. Yes No
- I was able to deliver my elevator speech comfortably. Yes No
- I was able to maintain eye contact for much of our discussion. Yes No

- I initiated an invitation to go out at a later date for coffee. Yes No
- I was comfortable/nervous in presenting my business card. Yes No
- I was comfortable in ending the conversation and moving on to another. Yes No
- I was able to ask some questions that moved the conversation forward. Yes No
- Overall I felt less or more nervous in comparison to other networking events. Yes No
- What did I learn about myself in this networking situation?

USING DEVELOPING BETTER PUBLIC SPEAKING SKILLS AS AN EXAMPLE, we find new speakers tend to focus on what they see as their shortcomings. Their shortcomings take on a life of their own and minimize the skills and talents that the speaker already has. Research has shown it is more effective to focus on the skills you already have and strengthen them rather than focusing on your own self-defined deficiencies. I believe the same thing applies to networking and conducting 1 to 1 conversations. Find out where your skills are and use them more.

Use the benchmark assessment after each event and reward yourself for areas you have shown improvement, especially those that have caused you considerable anxiety in the past.

So what if I do the assessment and I am still having a lot of anxiety? I am really nervous around people.

Shyness can be present in different degrees. Social anxiety can be a problem. I believe managing social situations is a skill that needs to be developed. When it comes to shyness or social anxiety, we are not born with well-developed social skills.

Your challenge is to reduce your anxiety to a manageable level. Having worked in the mental health field for over 30 years, often as nurse therapist, I'm not going to make a blanket statement to the effect of "get over it." There can be many causes of anxiety.

While I don't believe in Big Pharma's creating diagnoses such as "social anxiety" as a new market to sell their medications as a treatment, I do believe if your anxiety appears to be excessive, you really should have a talk with your doctor. There may be other reasons for your anxiety your doctor could help you with. Perhaps a mild anti-anxiety agent taken before you attend a networking session may help.

If your anxiety is excessive, there may be an advantage to you if you were to seek out some help from someone with a psychological background i.e. a psychologist. Sometimes we can use a little help in getting past some obstacles we have in life.

I had considered doing so at one point in my life to help me with interpersonal relationships but I chose a self-directed educational program instead. I found that one of my challenges was I hadn't developed many of the essential interpersonal skills at an early age.

As an adult I had to go back and learn the basics. My research exposed me to assertiveness training and communications, conflict and crisis management and systems thinking. As I mentioned earlier about having a tool box, the more skills & techniques you have in your repertoire the less likely you are to become overwhelmed in a situation. If I had to make a single recommendation to anyone as to the secret of leading a successful life I would have to recommend the different areas I researched. It certainly made my life easier.

Another technique I have used in developing my public speaking skills is that of using imagery. Before delivering a presentation to a group or a venue I'm not used to, I will go up to the front of the room i.e. where I will be delivering the speech from and I will imagine I am speaking.

I will imagine where everyone is seated. I will see their smiling faces and appreciation as to what I am saying. I see myself as being successful. So when I actually deliver my speech, I have already been successful in my mind.

This helps reduce the anxiety I might otherwise experience and allows me to focus on my delivery. The audience quite often doesn't react the same way in reality as they do in my imagination though. Five encores can be a little tiresome!

I believe the same technique can be used prior to participating in a networking event. Imagine yourself being successful, talking to different people and feeling confident. There is a Law of Attraction principle that addresses creating your own reality. So conversely, if you go to the event with the expectation you are going to have a stressful time, well then, guess what will happen?

In the next chapter we explore an overview of using social media for on-line networking.

ON-LINE NETWORKING: SOCIAL MEDIA OVERVIEW

Social Media Overview:

IN THIS CHAPTER WE EXPLORE SOCIAL MEDIA FOR ON-LINE networking.

Social media is here to stay. At least until the next latest and greatest bright shiny object comes along.

Developing an on-line presence and leveraging social media can be a great strategy in promoting and marketing yourself.

In most cases, your dominant personality traits won't be evident when you are on-line, unless your written language makes it obvious.

A quick on-line search to answer the question "what social media is good for networking?" revealed: Linkedin, Twitter and Instagram as being extraordinary tools for expanding and deepening your connections with business contacts, clients and potential partners.

Five tips to networking through social media are commonly identified:

- Build a social presence
- Post engaging content
- Avoid the hard sell
- Focus on quality over quantity
- Practice good etiquett.

Having been on social media for a while now I agree with the five points. In fact, they seem to be rather self-evident to me.

The development of different social media platforms and the ability to use them to market products or services has totally changed the face of marketing.

Many traditional marketers have had to incorporate on-line marketing strategies themselves to stay in business. A plethora of self-proclaimed marketing experts has been the result. Many of them will tell you that you absolutely need to be on social media and they have the skills and time to do it for you. For a fee of course!

While I whole-heartedly agree with Linkedin being recognized as a good on-line networking platform, maybe even the best, I don't agree with the suggestion of Twitter and Instagram being used for networking. Networking... 'no', self-promotion... 'yes.'

Leveraging social media is now within the reach of mere mortals. While I agree Twitter, Instagram and Facebook for that matter, provide value in promoting yourself, your products and your service, as I said, I don't agree with their value in networking.

Sure, you can connect with a lot of people and it looks impressive you have a massive number of connections but I ask 'are you really networking?'

I question the value of these connections. Twitter has evolved into a one-way data dump where everybody is pushing their content. As for meaningful conversations on Twitter, as far as I'm concerned... it's a joke.

I think Facebook is a great place to promote yourself however, I have many 'best friends' I have never met and am not likely to. Facebook has also morphed into a 'pay to play' venue where it will cost you for promotional activities.

While many individuals seem to continually draw attention to themselves, it is a little more challenging to promote your business without Facebook trying to sell you advertising.

I'm sure there are a lot of social media enthusiasts who will disagree with me. In light of our subject for discussion being 'power networking', I think you would be better off investing your time and energy in different places.

Power networking is about leveraging strategies to make you a better networker.

In the next section we look at promoting yourself if you are in job search mode. Even if you aren't... there are some good strategies offered here because you never know what the future brings.

> **"One of the marks of superior people is that they are action-oriented. One of the marks of average people is that they are talk-oriented." Brian Tracy**

> **"Refuse to criticize, condemn, or complain. Instead, think and talk only about the things you really want." Brian Tracy**

> **"Be a creator of circumstances rather than just a creature of circumstances. Be proactive rather than reactive." Brian Tracy**

PART III
SELF-PROMOTION WHEN JOB SEARCHING

SELF-PROMOTION WHEN JOB SEARCHING

In this section and upcoming chapters we look at promoting yourself if you are in job search mode.

If you are not in business for yourself, or you are working as a business professional in somebody else's business, you may find yourself looking for a job at some point in time.

If you are currently working in a job and don't have any plans to move on to something else, you may want to skip this chapter.

But then again, there are no certainties or guarantees to how long your employment will last. You may unexpectedly find you are job searching sooner rather than later.

This section provides generally accepted techniques to maximize your job searching effectiveness. The content for this chapter is excerpted from my book **You're Hired! Job Search Strategies That Work.**

In a competitive job hiring situation, it could come down to two or more possible candidates having very similar credentials and qualifications.

If there was ever a time that self-promotional skills and self-confidence would come into play, it would be in the job searching process.

Being able to effectively promote yourself can make the difference between landing the job and a "thank you very much, but we won't be hiring you at this time."

In the next chapter we look at how to create winning resumes.

∼

CREATING WINNING RESUMES

In this chapter, we look at techniques to create winning resumes. Let's start off with how to develop your content.

- Target your resume to the job.
- Start with a career summary.
- Summarize your experience, with the most recent employer and position first.
- If a strict chronological approach won't work for you, use a "combination" approach.
- Keep it short, no more than one page.
- Put the "hook" at the top.
- List only the more recent positions.
- Be consistent in how you list.
- Watch out for "time in job" problems.
- List education last.
- Keep it concise.
- Avoid "I ing" the reader to death.
- Begin sentences with strong action words that signal your effectiveness.

- Use your wonderful one page wisely.
- Emphasize results, not responsibilities.
- Avoid abbreviations.
- Write deliberately and edit.

Now let's look at some **Resume "Don'ts"**

- Don't upgrade or emphasize in handwritten notes.
- Don't include names of references.
- Don't state a salary.
- Don't state your objective.
- Don't give a reason for leaving previous jobs.
- Don't include a photograph.
- Don't apologize for self perceived "weaknesses."
- Don't editorialize.
- Don't overuse "buzzwords."
- Don't reveal your age or race.
- Don't mention firings or layoffs.
- Don't be sarcastic, humorous, or patronizing.
- Don't use gimmicks to get attention.
- Don't exaggerate or mislead.
- Don't send to the personnel department with a cover letter.
- Don't send your resume to "blind box" ads that don't reveal the employer's identity.
- Don't use a resume writing service.
- Don't state names of spouse or children.

Some more Major "Do's"

- Get a name for the envelope.
- If advantageous, bypass Human Resources completely.
- Consult an expert on grammar, spelling and punctuation.
- Emphasize individual accomplishments.

Creating the Style

BLOW YOUR OWN HORN!

- Use the power of white space.
- Have your resume typeset in no smaller than 10 point size.
- Use boldface and italic fonts sparingly.
- Print in black ink on quality white paper.
- Leave at least a 1-inch border all around.
- Center your name, address, and telephone number at the top.
- If space allows, include a few choice items of personal data at the bottom.
- Do not use all UPPER CASE letters

Think Marketing

- Have an objective.
- Think of the employer as a customer.
- Stress performance, not qualifications.
- Don't appear over-qualified.
- Time the arrival of the resume for the most attention.
- Use overnight delivery services in special cases, if a paper resume has been requested.
- Be prepared to e-mail or upload your resume to an on-line application portal in pdf format if requested.
- Follow up.

IN THE NEXT CHAPTER WE LOOK AT CREATING COVER LETTERS FOR job applications. Are they required or not? We will see...

"The winner's edge is not in a gifted birth, a high IQ, or in talent. The winner's edge is all in the attitude, not aptitude." **Denis Waitley**

Those who say winning isn't everything have probably never won anything. Anonymous

" If you don't invest very much, then defeat doesn't hurt very much and winning isn't very exciting." Dick Vermiel

CREATING COVER LETTERS

In this chapter we look at creating cover letters for job applications.

If you are applying on-line, you may or may not be able to use one.

Target your cover letter to the decision maker.

Address each letter completely with no abbreviations and include the middle initial and title of the recipient.

Use the proper spelling of all names and the correct company name. Call to check if you're not sure.

Don't precede the decision maker's name with "Mr.," "Ms.," or "Mrs." Do use the designation in the greeting of the letter, however. (Use "Mrs." only if you're sure the recipient does.)

In the greeting, don't address a decision maker by his or her first name.

Employ a simple writing style.

Limit the body of the letter to four paragraphs:

a. The introductory paragraph where the writer introduces himself or herself and mentions briefly how he or she knows you.

b. The value paragraph, which describes the applicant's background and highlights his or her attributes that will benefit the target company. It's the longest paragraph, but not more than five or six sentences. It should be sincere and persuasive.

c. The action paragraph, which asks the reader to read the resume enclosed and contact the applicant for an interview (or wait patiently for him or her to call.)

d. The closing paragraph, which expresses appreciation.

Don't attach a cover letter to a resume going to the personnel department.

In our next chapter we revisit leveraging and building your network in relation to job searching.

∽

> "Follow your instincts. That's where true wisdom manifests itself." Oprah Winfrey

> "Dare to go forward! Have you ever tried pushing a string?" Brian Tracy

> "Most people engage in activities that are tension-relieving rather than goal-achieving." Brian Tracy

YOUR NETWORK WEB

In this chapter we revisit leveraging and building your network in relation to job searching.

Step One is to make a list of your personal categories.

These are your interests and the organizations, formal and informal you belong to.

These may include hobbies, family, church, professional organizations, sports teams, current and past employment.

Step Two is to make a list of people you know in each category, start with a list of 10 names for each organization or interest category, and then add 10 more if possible.

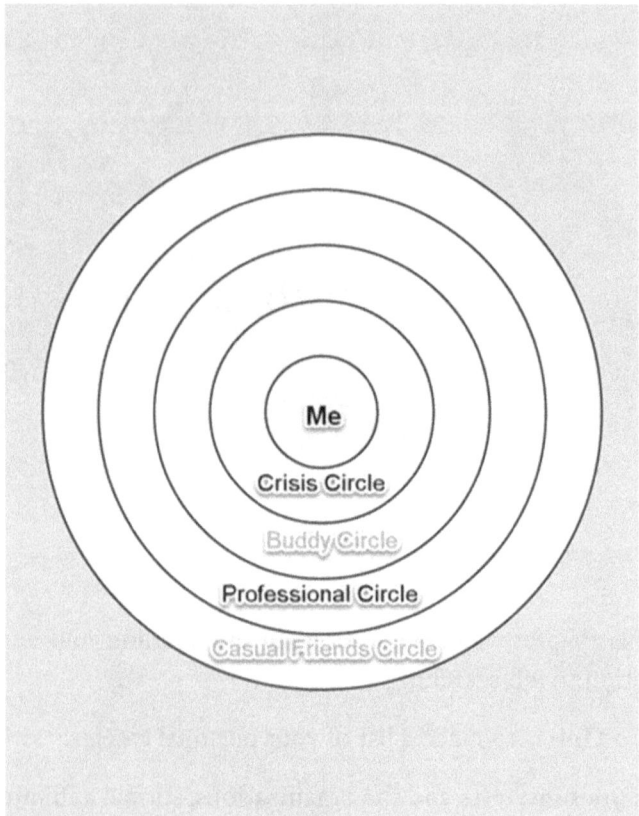

Step Three is to create a web on a piece of paper with the following four circles:

First Circle: The crisis circle is closest to the center of the Web.

These are the people you can really count on.

You should have at least four people who will be supportive in the event of death, illness, divorce or bankruptcy.

They can include family, friends, your doctor or lawyer.

The Second Circle: This is your buddy circle.

Friends you have fun with, the people who accept you for who you are.

There should be at least three people in this circle.

The Third Circle: This is your professional circle.

People who, you know professionally, can provide reference letters, and can speak about the quality of your work and character.

You need at least 12 people in this category.

The Fourth Circle: This is your casual friends circle.

People you can share ideas with.

You may work with them or know them through organizations or volunteer work.

Some may become closer friends and eventually form part of the more inner and intimate circles.

Up, to this point we haven't factored in our Linkedin connections. Likely, many of your Linkedin connections will fit into your Third Circle, your professional circle.

The *Network Web* is a powerful tool. You'll be amazed at all the contacts you do have, and can identify the gaps in the network.

With your goal in mind, you can ask:

Who do I need to know?

Who do I need to bring into my circle?

And who do I know that can introduce them to me?

IN THE NEXT CHAPTER WE LOOK AT JOB SEARCHING STRATEGIES TO promote yourself starting with the initial job interview phone call.

THE INITIAL INTERVIEW PHONE CALL

In this chapter we look at job searching strategies to promote yourself starting with the initial job interview phone call.

Your resume wowed them! They want to speak with you in person. Now what?

The interview process starts from the very first phone call the prospective employer makes to arrange for an interview.

Be prepared! You are being judged!

Your telephone answering machine or voice mail, should have an appropriate, professional sounding greeting.

When you are job searching, it isn't the time to have a catchy novelty telephone greeting.

Have pen & paper at the ready.

Have easy access to your personal agenda or commitments so that you can readily arrange for an interview appointment.

Here are some questions to ask while you have them on the phone or in an e-mail if that was their initial contact method:

- time & location?
- who will be conducting the interview?
- what format will the interview be?
- are there other people being interviewed for the job?
- is there anything that you need to bring with you?

Here are some interview formats you may encounter:

- individual interviewer
- team interview (panel)
- team with other applicants
- on camera

Will Rogers said, "I never met a man I didn't like."

An employment interview is a place to be liked.

Unless you're likeable, you won't be hireable.

In our next chapter, we revisit dressing for success from a job searching perspective.

"Networking is simply the cultivating of mutually beneficial, give and take, win-win relationships. It works best, however, when emphasizing the 'give' part." Bob Burg

Network continually... 85 percent of all jobs are filled through contacts and personal references." Brian Tracy

DRESS FOR SUCCESS REVISITED

In this chapter we revisit dressing for success from a job searching perspective.

When job hunting, dress for success.

In job-hunting, first impressions are critical.

Remember, you are marketing a product... yourself... to a potential employer.

And the first thing the employer sees when greeting you is your attire.

Therefore, you must make every effort to have the proper dress for the type of job you are seeking.

The old saying 'never judge a book by its cover' may be a good one, but interviewers are human like everybody else and likely to act upon their first impressions.

So, you want to make sure you are giving a good one.

In our next chapter we look at preparing to answer interview questions.

"Networking is simply the cultivating of mutually beneficial, give and take, win-win relationships. It works best, however, when emphasizing the 'give' part." Bob Burg

Network continually... 85 percent of all jobs are filled through contacts and personal references." Brian Tracy

ORGANIZING YOUR PRESENTATION

This chapter is on **Organizing Your Presentation** and offers tips on how to answer job interview questions.

Here are some sure-fire formulas of organizing your responses to the interviewer's questions.

Past, Present, Future

Here is an example, "In the past I would have handled the situation this way..."

"Recently I experienced a similar situation and this is how I handled it..."

"I learned from it and here is how I would handle it should I encounter it again..."

Here's another possible outline - Problem/Cause/Solution

- "The problem is..."
- "The problem is caused by..."
- "Some solutions are..."
- "The best solution is..."

Dale Carnegie's Magic Formula

Example, point, reason.

Example: Give details of an incident that graphically illustrates your main idea.

Point: Tell exactly what you want your audience to do.

Reason: Highlight the advantage or benefit to be gained when they do what you ask them to.

EVERY PRESENTATION, REGARDLESS OF ITS LENGTH, SHOULD have these three components:

- Opening
- Body
- Closing

LET'S TAKE A LOOK AT THE JOB INTERVIEW PROCESS, STARTING OFF with your first interview.

In my part of the world where we have a tight job market, just getting to the interview stage can be like winning a lottery.

Your resume likely got you to the interview stage.

The goal for this first face-to-face encounter is to win a second interview or to be hired right away.

Tell yourself beforehand you need to come away with a good sense of the most effective techniques and timing for this target.

Then when you are inside the prospective employer's office:

Be Observant

Throughout the interview, look and listen to gather information that will help you.

A successful interview requires the ability to think on your feet.

Undivided attention is necessary to seize opportunities as they arise.

Take Out Your Well Organized Notebook and Jot Down Notes

It makes you look professional.

Write names, titles, buzzwords, products, and other items you can use in the follow up stage.

Don't reduce your eye contact with the Interviewer; don't ask him or her to repeat anything or how to spell something.

You can and should ask questions.

Not only do the right questions help you control the interview, but by asking them, you elicit information to fuel your follow up.

Ask the right questions.

Don't ask personal controversial or negative questions of any kind.

Stay away from asking anything that will lead into sensitive areas.

Invariably salary and benefits should be avoided.

Nowadays, you can often gather quite a bit of information about the organization you are applying to by doing a search on the Internet.

It will be expected you have some understanding of their business.

While some knowledge will certainly be helpful, a lack of knowledge or asking questions you should already know the answers to, could work against you.

Here are examples of benign questions that may have a favorable impact:

- How many employees does the company have?
- What are the company's plans for expansion?
- Is the business operated as a proprietorship or a non-profit?

- What is the supervisor's management style?
- What is the supervisor's title?
- Who does the supervisor report to?
- Are you ready and able to hire now?
- How long will it take to make a hiring decision?
- How long has the position been open?
- How many employees have held the position in the past five years?
- Why are the former employees no longer in the position?
- What does the company consider the five most important duties of the position to be?
- What do you expect the employee you hire to accomplish?

Jot some keywords and concepts from these questions and answers into a page of a small notebook.

Now we are going to prepare to use some tactics that will turn the interview in your favor.

Here is a job interview checklist that aims at helping you with that.

Job Interview Checklist

Interview "Do's"

- Schedule for success.
- Avoid meal interviews.
- Arrive alone and on time. Don't arrive early. Acclimate to your environment.
- Carry an attaché case.
- Eliminate fear of the unknown.
- Make the first impression the best.
- Greet the interviewer properly.
- Hone your handshake.
- Avoid assuming a subordinate role.

- Have your script well-rehearsed.
- Attempt to sit next to or near the interviewer.
- Take notes.
- Have an extra copy of your resume with you in case the interviewer doesn't have it.
- Educational background questions: Show what you know!
- Character questions: Be careful!
- Initiative and creativity questions: Focus on what and why.
- Career and objective questions: Make it clear what they hear.
- Admire something in the interviewer's office.

Assess the interviewer's style.

- "Mirror" the interviewer's body language, facial expressions, eye movement, rate of speech, tone of voice and rate of breathing.
- Align with the interviewer.
- Use "insider" language.
- Find an area of agreement and lead slowly and carefully to the offer.
- Be honest, not modest.
- Say positive things about your present (former) employer.
- Admire the achievements of the prospective employer.
- Be observant.
- Review your notes.
- Limit interview to two hours.
- At the end of the interview, thank them for their time, shake hands again, and tell them you hope to hear from them soon.

THESE ARE ALL FACTORS TO TAKE INTO CONSIDERATION TO HELP YOU become the successful job applicant.

Of course, you still have to wow them with your interview question answers.

. . .

WE JUST LOOKED AT SOME STRATEGIES WE *SHOULD* DO IN preparation and during the interview.

Now let's take a look at some interview **Don'ts.**

INTERVIEW "DON'TS"

- Don't wear a coat, hat, or other outdoor clothing into the interview.
- Don't wait more than half an hour for the interviewer.
- Don't address the interviewer by his or her first name.
- Don't use trite phrases and/or tired clichés.
- Don't smoke.
- Don't chew gum.
- Don't interrupt.
- Don't object to discriminatory questions.
- Don't look at your watch.
- Don't read any documents on the interviewer's desk.

IT LOOKS LIKE THERE ARE A LOT FEWER THINGS YOU SHOULDN'T BE doing than what you should be doing.

IN THE NEXT CHAPTER WE LOOK AT THE FOLLOW-UP JOB INTERVIEW phone call.

> **Christopher Robinson on Organization in Winnie the Pooh.** "Organizing is what you do before you do something, so that when you do it, it's not all mixed up."

> "You cannot change your destination overnight, but you can change your direction overnight." **Jim Rohn**

THE FOLLOW-UP JOB INTERVIEW PHONE CALL

In this chapter we look at the follow-up job interview phone call.

The Follow-up Telephone Call

Assuming you have made it to the interview stage, here is a strategy to consider using after your interview.

The follow-up telephone call is one of the most important devices in the job search --- and also one of the most unused.

Many job searchers don't feel confident enough about themselves to make this important phone call.

As with your initial follow-up response, the keys to success when you telephone your target are timing and technique. That means knowing:

- When to call
- Whom to call
- And What to say

Your ongoing purpose of this follow-up phone call is to maintain the prospect's impression of you as:

- Enthusiastic
- Confident
- Energetic
- Dependable
- Loyal
- Honest
- Proud of your work
- Concerned with service

The fact that you're taking the trouble to make this follow-up call, by itself, demonstrates these qualities.

Or at least it should!

Let's look at timing the Telephone Follow-up.

Don't Wait Too Long!

The best advice to heed is the "fiddle theory," introduced by Robert Singer in Winning Through Intimidation:

The longer a person fiddles around with something, the greater the odds the result will be negative...

In the case of Nero, Rome burned; in the case of a sale, the longer it takes to get to a point of closing, the greater the odds it will never close.

As a general rule, you should always assume that time is always against you when you try to make a deal --- any kind of deal.

There's an old saying about "striking while the iron's hot."

If you haven't received a response to your follow-up letter within a week after the interview, call, but... **Never on a Monday.**

Mondays are full of staff meetings, unexpected crises, and weekend wounds. Don't call, write, or interview on a Monday if you can help it.

Statistically, the best time to call is Tuesday through Friday, from 9.00 am to 11.00 am.

Targeting the Telephone Follow-up

You already know who should receive your call. You spent a long time talking with him or her during the first interview.

Despite the interview tips, you may still feel in a one-down position with your interviewer. Don't!

Initiating the call automatically gives you the upper hand. You're prepared and can guide the conversation to the outcome you want.

IN THE NEXT CHAPTER WE LOOK AT FOUR BASIC INTERVIEWER personality types and offer strategies to deal with them.

BASIC INTERVIEWER PERSONALITY TYPES

In this chapter, we look at how to recognize Four Basic Personality Types you might encounter in a job interview and offer strategies to deal with them.

There are likely several models out there, but this one seems to work well.

Type 1 are Outgoing and Direct:

These people are called "socializers." They are energetic, friendly, and self assured.

To spot this personality, look for the following characteristics:

1. A flamboyant style of dress. Even in a conservative business suit, a brightly colored tie, scarf, or jewelery might be worn. Current fashion is preferred to classic styles.

2. They likely have many pictures and personal mementos in the office.

3. They will have a cluttered desk, or at least a covered one.

4. They aren't very time conscious, so you might be kept waiting. In most cases, the Interviewer is juggling a hundred things at once. These

types gravitate toward personnel jobs because they're outgoing 'people' people.

If you're a methodical, reserved type, you can get into trouble with Interviewers of this type. You'll have to smile, talk faster, and get to the point.

They have to like you before they'll listen to you. And listening isn't on their list.

If you're this type, be careful. You don't want to out talk, out smile or out interview the Interviewer!

The second interviewer personality type is referred to as the 'director.' 'Dictator' is more descriptive, though.

These people differ from socializers because they're far more reserved and conservative.

Before unconventional computer kids started running companies, it was believed you had to be like this to make top management. They're still among the high achievers in every field.

Clues to this personality are:

1. They have a conservative, high quality, custom tailored wardrobe, impeccably worn.

2. They have a neat, organized work space. A few expensive personal desk accessories.

Perhaps one or two classic picture frames containing family photos. Nothing flashy. Everything is understated.

3. They have a firm handshake, but not much of a smile. Not as talkative as the first type. They'll size you up critically and wait for you to make your mistakes.

4. Time conscious and annoyed when others are not. They are goal, and bottom line oriented. They believe that all work and no play is the way to spend the day.

BLOW YOUR OWN HORN!

To get along with this type, be all business. Don't waste the Interviewer's time. Eliminate unnecessary words and be sincere.

This type itches around "touchy feely" people. You won't find them saying, "Oh, I just adore this." You shouldn't either.

Don't be intimidated, either. If you are, Director types will sense it and reject you immediately. Don't be defensive about weaknesses in your background. Just explain them by turning them into strengths.

Next is the third Interviewer personality type.

Such people are called 'thinkers' and might be found in analytical professions. They don't speak up, socialize, or editorialize. They go about their work quietly, and they get it done properly.

Evidence of this personality includes:

1. Uninteresting understated clothes. Gray and beige predominate. Style and looks aren't a priority, function is. The person is nothing if not practical.

2. They have few personal items and 'warm fuzzies.'

3. This Interviewer's hand will probably dangle at the end of their wrist. Shake it any way. It will confirm your suspicions that he or she is a 'thinker.'

4. They are time conscious and work oriented. Their work ethic is just as strong as the Directors', but Thinkers don't want to run things, they are loners.

5. They will likely have an organized desk, with neatly arranged work. Maybe even a 'to do' list with half the items crossed off.

This type of person is hard to draw out and may become annoyed if you try. If you're pushy and aggressive, the thinker gets withdrawn and your offer will be withheld.

Answer questions directly and succinctly. Volunteer as much information as the Interviewer needs to make a decision. Thinkers thrive on data, but they need time to analyze it, so don't rush.

Next, we look at the fourth Interviewer personality type.

The most common word for this personality type is 'helper.' They're friendly, like socializers, but without the aggressiveness.

Helpers tend to gravitate toward 'human resources' they're the closest the business world gets to providing psychiatric social work for employees. Helpers take time to know you before the actual interview begins.

They're nice, but will do almost anything to avoid making a decision. In that area, you need to help them.

You're probably talking to a helper when there is:

1. A nonthreatening appearance that matches their demeanor. They wear natural shades and soft fabrics.

2. They have a number of personal items on the desk, often handmade. Their office will reflect that other people are important to them.

3. They have a friendly, expressive, and concerned approach. Helpers may apologize for keeping you waiting because they were busy solving everyone else's problems.

They smile warmly, reach out to take your hand, and might never let it go.

4. They will likely have a phone ringing, work piling up, and many uncompleted projects. To a helper, 'people' are all that matters.

These people are the opposite of the 'director' type, and they rarely play opposite each other.

The helper never gives up trying to convince the director to 'humanize,' 'personalize,' and 'realize.'

To get hired, take time to establish rapport, become friends, and accentuate the importance of the 'person' in 'personnel.' But remember to limit interviews to two hours.

With helpers, it's your responsibility to get your job qualifications across. If you don't, you may leave the interview with a friend but not a job.

They won't ask you to give them a reason to hire you or even recommend you for a second interview. Emotionally, they don't realize that's why you're there. They think it's because you're taking a hiring survey. A helper helps... but doesn't hire.

This is a remarkably accurate way to out stereotype the stereotypers. Some will fit the description exactly, others will fit several.

No matter. Just know and play to your audience. Study the four profiles and practice typecasting a few of your friends, coworkers, and relatives.

Learn to pick up on the clues to someone's predominant personality style. Then practice playing to them. They're your audience, too.

Picking up clues from a person's appearance, speech, and body language can serve you in many ways throughout your career. In short, while you are concentrating on making a good impression, you also need to be absorbing a clear impression of everybody and everything else.

IN THE NEXT SECTION WE FOCUS ON ON-LINE STRATEGIES FOR personal branding & marketing.

~

PART IV
ON-LINE STRATEGIES FOR PERSONAL BRANDING & MARKETING

ON-LINE REPUTATION MANAGEMENT

In this section we focus on on-line strategies for personal branding & marketing starting off with reputation management.

SOCIAL MEDIA IS HERE TO STAY!

At least until the next latest and greatest on-line venue grabs our attention.

In upcoming chapters, we explore several social media platforms and how they relate to promoting your personal brand, on-line.

We will also explore tactics for protecting your on-line reputation .

There are some very nasty people out there!

Think damage control.

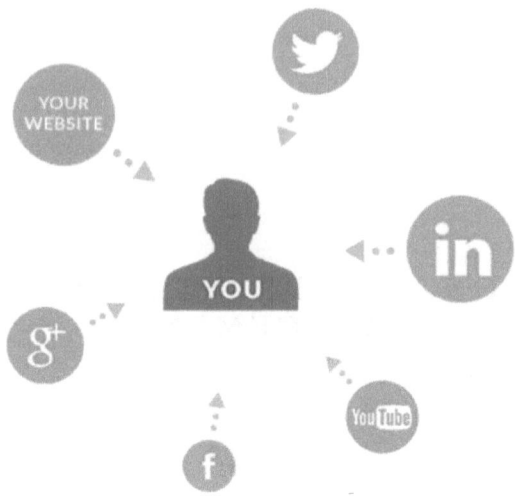

In this chapter we look closely at on-line reputation management.

Throughout this book we have been focusing on how to effectively promote yourself.

The Internet and arguably many of the social media venues hosted on the Internet can be great places to market and promote yourself.

It comes with a cost though. It takes time, energy and sometimes money to make it work for you.

While it's quite easy to upload something to the Internet, it can work against you.

Anything you post to the Internet will likely be there forever. Forever is a very long time!

Then there is the problem of what other people post about you. That becomes a little more challenging to deal with, but it can be done.

Here is a quick systematic approach to managing your on-line reputation.

Have you Googled yourself lately? It's probably as good a first step as any.

But before you do so, there is a bit of a trick involved to make it accurate.

There's a couple steps you need to take first.

Firstly, sign out of your Google Account if you are logged in.

Regardless of what browser you are using, make sure you have signed out of your personal Google Account, cleared your browsing history, cache and cookies.

Or if you can, open an incognito window.

The reason we do this is to get results that are as unbiased as possible.

Google keeps track of your searches and other characteristics of your browsing history and alters result rankings depending on who is searching and where the user is located.

The next step is to type your name into the search bar.

Now here's a few notes about that.

When you are first assessing your Google results, make sure you are typing in the name other people will use when they search for you.

Use your professional name.

Consistency is important, so when you use your name on a business card, on-line or really anywhere, make things easy for yourself and use the same name.

Think of this name as the center of your on-line reputation.

Once you've Googled yourself, it's time to take a hard look at your results.

Evaluate these results to see just what kind of information is out there about you.

. . .

Next we are going to look at three categories that may apply to you.

As we go through them try to determine which category best describes your search results.

The first one can be called the '**Negative Category**':

As you would expect, this is the worst category to be in because one or more negative results are representing you on-line.

In today's world of social networking and anonymous sharing, bad search results can happen to good people at any time.

It is disturbingly easy to have your reputation tarnished.

It takes only one status update, tagged photo or blog post from a disgruntled former employee to put you in this category.

A second category can be described as the "**That's Not Me!**" Category.

This category is reserved for results that are dominated by someone else (or multiple people) with the same name as yours.

This scenario blocks others from finding out relevant or accurate information about you.

In a worst-case scenario, users might mistake you for someone else.

I recall years ago, long before the Internet, my uncle and another local fellow shared the same name.

The other fellow always seemed to be in trouble.

When he would get arrested or committed to our local psychiatric hospital, it would be featured in the newspapers.

Many people assumed it was my uncle who had the bad reputation.

The same phenomena as what my uncle experienced can easily occur on-line.

A third category may be called "**That is Me!**" Category.

This is the good one. This is the one you want to be in.

Ideally you want the results associated with your name to be well-branded, relevant and display positive content about you.

If this is the case, you must be doing something right.

But remember maintaining a *positive* and *relevant* status takes work, so you need to continue to be consistent about actively maintaining your social media profiles and websites.

Here's a tip from the Pros.

While many people think the first page of Google and other search engines are the most important, it's critical to see what kinds of properties are populating the second and third pages too.

If you control any of the properties listed there, you can use it your advantage in months to come.

Google at the time of writing this owns about 75% of the search engine traffic. It would be worth your while to conduct research on your name on other popular search engines, just to be sure about what is out there.

LET'S CONTINUE ON WITH THE ASSESSING YOUR ON-LINE PRESENCE A little longer.

Regardless of your interpretation of your assessment, you need to be proactive to improve or maintain your on-line presence.

Now we are going to look at some suggestions for your next steps, based on your current situation.

Let's start off with a quick overview of three different scenarios.

We'll expand upon them a little later so that we don't make it too confusing.

In the case you *Have No Web Presence, and No Content,* then there is no way for it to show up on the first page search engine results or any other page for that matter.

When I encounter somebody by way of my business networking activities, I often Google them to find out more info about them.

As a moderator for several Facebook groups, I am selective as to who I allow join a group.

One of the first things I do is to Google the individual to find out what I can about them.

When I don't find anything or very little, I get suspicious.

That's just me though.

It may not be the norm, but many people are conducting on-line reputation searches.

If somebody has reason to research your name, perhaps you have applied for a job, you want to ensure they find something positive about you.

So, in this case, the first thing you need to do is build up your on-line presence.

We'll go into more depth on how to do so a little later.

Another possible situation is where you have *Negative Results that are Damaging Your Reputation.*

Maybe there is something out there that is unflattering and untrue about you, or perhaps you're also being mistaken for someone who does have a bad reputation.

This isn't as uncommon a situation as you might think it is.

Several years back I had a cyberstalker, who had the intention of damaging my reputation.

She didn't, but she was persistent.

In the next chapter I go into greater detail on the subject and the actions I had taken at the time.

The short version is she tried to tarnish my reputation by threatening me on several social media platforms.

She also took a series of photos of herself, in the nude, brandishing medieval weaponry, at various locations around our town.

One picture was of her nude, on a hilltop, swaying a large sword over her head with the caption "I'm going to get you Rae Stonehouse..."

Hopefully, you won't come across a person that is as deranged as this one, but they are out there!

We will talk about what to do in this situation to reduce the effect to your on-line reputation a little later.

We are still talking about different scenarios your on-line presence may fall into.

A third situation may be where you have *Specific Content You Want to Push Higher* in the search engine results.

You might already have a personal website, a LinkedIn profile, blogs or other content you want people to find, but they just aren't showing up very high in search results.

We will explore search engine optimization in an upcoming chapter.

The next step in your on-line reputation management is to create a plan and put it into action.

We'll start off by jump starting your on-line presence.

If you haven't already, purchase your domain (yourname.com).

Domain Registrars are easy enough to find on-line.

You can lock in your personal name, assuming somebody else hasn't already done so, without having to immediately upload a website to it.

Purchasing your domain name is quite possibly the most important step you can take in gaining control of your on-line presence.

At only $10 to $20 dollars per year (more or less) depending on which country you live in, purchasing your domain name is an investment opportunity you can't afford to miss.

To buy your domain, you can visit any number of registrars on-line.

Try to get access to your own name, that is the name you want to be known by and be searchable.

Your name will become your *keyword*, which is a basic concept for search engine results.

Another decision to make is what extension should you purchase?

If you are in business, going with a dot com extension still appears to be of value.

For whatever reason, the dot com extension gives the illusion you and your business are professional.

I personally own about 30 or so web domains.

If the website is business related, I will buy the dot com extension.

I live in Canada and I believe that there is value in promoting the .ca extension, ca being for Canada.

As an example, I own raestonehouse.ca and raestonehouse.com to promote myself as an author and my other ventures.

I have a website set up on one of the domain addresses and the other is set up as a forwarder to it, should somebody type the other one in.

The visitor will end up on my site, one way or another.

Registering and owning your own domain name will require yearly ongoing payments.

But it is likely a small price to pay for the benefits it offers and the protection from others getting to it first might cause.

So what do you do if somebody with the same name as yours beats you to the punch, that is, they have purchased your domain name before you have?

For people with fairly common names, this may happen easily.

You will likely have to get creative at this point.

Perhaps adding your city or town to the end of your name might help to differentiate you from all the other people with the same name.

In my case instead of raestonehouse.ca I could go with raestonehouse-kelowna.ca.

Kelowna is the city I currently live in.

If I were to move to another city, I would have to change the name of the city in my domain name, which might cause some problems with future search engine results.

Fortunately for me, I appear to be the one and only Rae Stonehouse, so I haven't experienced that problem.

RAISING THE BAR A LITTLE IN COMPLEXITY, THE NEXT STEP IN OUR on-line reputation management plan is to build a personal website.

Once you have purchased your domain, it's time to build a personal website on the web where you can display everything from your work history to your personal interests.

It's your website, so you can post what you want.

Bearing in mind whatever you post has to be consistent with the image you want to portray.

You still have to think marketing and promotion.

Once upon a time website development was only doable by highly skilled and expensive experts. It wasn't within the reach of us mere mortals.

Today, almost anybody can create their own personal website, without having advanced technical knowledge.

Content management systems (CMS) have made it relatively easy to get a professional-looking website up and running.

There are a lot of options out there, but WordPress seems to be the most recommended for ease of use by beginners.

It's relatively easy to get set up and also allows for customization as you develop your personal identity on-line.

This means you have the option of changing the look and structure of the site as you get more familiar with how WordPress works.

Going into more depth on how to actually develop your website is beyond the scope of this book.

However, there is a wealth of tutorial advice on-line to help with your learning curve.

In the last section we talked about how creating your own website is an important step in developing a strong foundation for your on-line presence.

The next step in our plan to create your on-line presence is to get on social networks, that is, if you aren't already.

Social media can play an important role in directing traffic to your personal website.

Social media also seems to be an ever-changing environment.

What is hot today may not be in the upcoming days, months and years.

Facebook, Linkedin, Instagram and Twitter seem to have some staying power.

From my perspective, social media can take over your every waking moment, if you let it.

Along with a dozen or so active websites, I also own about a dozen Twitter profiles and close to ten Facebook properties.

Lets just say creating them all seemed like a good idea at the time.

I tend to focus only on a few of them right now as my creative ideas tend to take me all over the place.

When it comes to search engine results, some engines seem to do a better job at indexing your posts better than others do.

If you consistently share and write quality information, your chances of getting your content indexed increases.

As an effective strategy, you are probably better to get involved on a social media platform where the people you want to meet and associate with hang out.

While social media can be fun, it can definitely suck your spare time away from you, so caution is advised.

From an on-line reputation management perspective, the value of social media participation is of helping to create your on-line expertise.

The postings and content you upload should work towards enhancing your on-line reputation, not take away from it.

I HAVE HAD GOOD LUCK WITH A SOCIAL MEDIA VENUE CALLED Quora.com.

The concept behind Quora is there are other valid forms of education besides formalized education.

Sage advice from people who really do know the answer has good value.

The basic premise is it is free to join. If you have a question, you post it.

Self-proclaimed experts have the opportunity to provide their sage advice on whatever the question is.

At the time of writing this content, I have been one of those self-proclaimed experts for about several years now. I expand upon Quora in an upcoming chapter.

Continuing on with our plan of on-line reputation management, another step, though not necessarily the next step, is to take advantage of filling out on-line profiles.

Any social media venue you join will likely require you to fill out a profile.

From their perspective, I'm sure it sets you up to be marketed to.

There is a slight possibility that your profile will get indexed by search engines.

One advantage of these on-line profiles is you can list the URL for your domain name, that you want to draw traffic to.

One thing to keep in mind is if you are posting profiles to multiple different locations, there should be similarity in what you post.

Meaning that your Bio should be consistent.

I have been writing blog articles for several years now, and they appear on many of my websites.

I had been using different bios over the years but have recently settled on the one that I created as my Amazon Author Bio for all of my published books.

How do you keep track of what is posted to the Internet about you?

You can easily Google yourself at any time to see what is new.

Google allows you to fine tune the time frame of its search.

If you click on *Tools* in the navigational bar, then on *Anytime*, it will give you several choices of times.

I tend to check myself out once a month using the *Past Month* selection.

Another technique for more frequent monitoring is to create a Google Alert.

They are quite easy to set up.

Type in google.com/alerts in your browser.

Then enter your name as the search term for the topic you want to track. Then choose *Show Options* to narrow the alert to a specific source, language, and/or region.

Finally you click on *Create Alert* to activate it.

Yet another area we need to keep tabs on within search engines is that of their images collections.

Search engines collect copies of graphics that are connected to you in some way.

Sometimes you have to wonder about the connection though.

If your name is listed as part of the graphics attributes, likely the graphic will get indexed under your name.

If a photo is tagged on social media, odds are it will be indexed under the *Images* section.

If you use graphics on your website or blog, it will likely be indexed and attributed to you.

If you are using graphics, you want to make sure you have permission to use the graphic.

It would be a nasty situation if you were to receive a cease and desist usage request over a photo you used that belonged to someone else.

This could also very well come with a request to pay the owner anywhere from 5 to 10 thousand dollars to the owner, to teach you a lesson.

It could happen. Don't let it. Give proper credit where credit is due.

As to dealing with pictures of yourself that someone else has taken and posted to social media, it can be challenging to keep on top of.

You may be totally unaware of a photo that got uploaded to social media. If it shows you in a less than flattering light, you may want to ask the poster to remove the photo.

It really would be rough if there was a photo of you out there that a potential employer found, causing them to say "No Way I'm hiring this person!"

You really do need to be proactive and check out your on-line presence on a regular basis, even if you think that you don't have one.

Social media is here to stay!

At least until the next latest and greatest on-line venue grabs our attention.

In upcoming chapters, we explore several social media platforms and how they relate to promoting your personal brand, on-line.

We will also explore tactics for protecting your on-line reputation.

There are some very nasty people out there!

Think damage control.

In the next chapter we explore cyber bullying, how to recognize it and what to do about it.

Action Items:

1. Set your browser up for an unbiased search engine search as described in this chapter.
2. Search various search engines for the name that you want to be found as.
3. Create and follow a schedule of routinely 'googling' yourself.

"I've always tried to live with the following simple rule; 'Don't do what you would feel uncomfortable reading about in the newspaper the next day." Josh Weston, chairman and CEO of Automatic Data Processing Inc.

"Deal honestly and objectively with yourself; intellectual honesty and personal courage are the hallmarks of great character." Brian Tracy

"Each of us must be committed to maintaining the reputation of all of us. And all of us must be committed to maintaining the reputation of each of us." Jim Rohn

CYBERBULLYING PREVENTION STRATEGIES

In this chapter we explore cyberbullying, how to recognize it and what to do about it.

IF YOU ARE ACTIVELY MARKETING AND PROMOTING YOURSELF ONline as a part of your networking efforts, the likelihood of encountering a cyber bully increases exponentially. It's simply a matter of numbers, the more people you network with the higher the odds of encountering one.

Cyberbullying has featured prominently lately in the media with the unfortunate suicides of several teens in North America. As adults, we aren't immune to the same tactics, these bullies use.

So what is a 'cyberbully'?

From Wikipedia, the free encyclopedia... *Cyberbullying* is the use of the Internet and related technologies to harm other people, in a deliberate, repeated, and hostile manner.

Cyberbullying is defined in legal glossaries as:

BLOW YOUR OWN HORN!

- actions that use information and communication technologies to support deliberate, repeated, and hostile behavior by an individual or group, that is intended to harm another or others.
- use of communication technologies for the intention of harming another person
- use of Internet service and mobile technologies such as web pages and discussion groups as well as instant messaging or SMS text messaging with the intention of harming another person.

Examples of what constitutes cyberbullying include communications that seek to intimidate, control, manipulate, put down, falsely discredit, or humiliate the recipient. The actions are deliberate, repeated, and hostile behaviour intended to harm another. Cyberbullying has been defined by The National Crime Prevention Council: "When the Internet, cell phones or other devices are used to send or post text or images intended to hurt or embarrass another person."

The practice of cyberbullying is not limited to children and, while the behavior is identified by the same definition when practiced by adults, the distinction in age groups sometimes refers to the abuse as cyberstalking or cyberharassment when perpetrated by adults toward adults.

Common tactics used by cyberstalkers are performed in public forums, social media or online information sites and are intended to threaten a victim's earnings, employment, reputation, or safety. Behaviors may include encouraging others to harass the victim and trying to affect a victim's on-line participation. Many cyberstalkers try to damage the reputation of their victim and turn other people against them.**Source:** Wikipedia... Cyberbullying & Cyberstalking.

A cyberbully could be a complete stranger to you or someone you know.

This chapter's content was a result of having dealt with a cyberbully over a five-month period, one that I have never actually met in person. I would like to share some cyberbullying prevention strategies I have learned during my journey so you don't have to go through the misery. And that dear reader is what the bully wants. They want you to be miserable. Your misery is their goal.

My experience began innocently enough when I cautioned a poster to a Facebook Group page I moderated. The individual had added their comments to a post I had made and side-tracked the conversation. As the Moderator I felt the content posted was inappropriate for a public forum as it was harassing another member of the group and making veiled threats.

I advised the individual that firstly, I felt the content they posted was inappropriate for a public forum. Secondly, their dispute was with an individual and they should deal with them directly. Thirdly, I made myself available for discussion of this matter and should they continue further in this manner I would be obligated to revoke their membership from the Facebook group.

In their self-righteous indignation they quickly posted several more posts, however this time they were directed at me. As I had previously cautioned them, I followed through and revoked their membership to the group page which in turn deleted the comments to the post.

Thinking the incident was over, I was dismayed to find a tirade of accusations posted on their Twitter feed about me. I then found I was highlighted on their website's blog as being the scourge of mankind as well as attacked on their personal Facebook page. I like attention as much as the next guy, but this was out of control!

The intent of this chapter is not to get into the "he said"... "she said" details of this situation, but to learn from it.

I had worked some 33 years as a Registered Nurse in the field of psychiatry/mental health at the time, and through those years I believe I have developed a good understanding of human behaviour. At least I am able to recognize behaviour that does not fall within the parameters of so-called normal behaviour.

Over the next few paragraphs I will endeavor to provide some background info on why bullies bully from a psychological perspective. It isn't a one size fits all profile but I would challenge you to think about people you know or have encountered and determine if they fall into any of these categories.

Some people display paranoid personality traits without meeting all the criteria of being diagnosed as a paranoid personality disorder.

Common characteristics of a paranoid individual are as follows: suspiciousness (looking for hidden reasons, meanings, causes etc. to another's behaviour and/or actions); hypervigilance i.e. being super aware of situations that they feel could cause them harm; short-tempered and lack of trust.

The individual bullying you may have paranoia and for whatever reasons have chosen you as a target.

Working in mental health for so many years I learned an adage that has served me well... 'all behaviour has meaning.' The challenge is in determining what the meaning of the behaviour is and what it is supposed to do for the individual displaying it.

A cyberbully displays the same characteristics of a bully in the 'real world.' They usually have inadequate personalities, poor interpersonal skills, poor coping skills and a lack of empathy. They seek out individuals who they feel that by dominating them, they can raise their stature.

I recall a book written back in the 1970s entitled *The Games People Play* by a psychologist named Eric Berne. Berne outlined different interpersonal transactions people have with each other, calling them 'games'. Ideally, as adults respectful of each other we communicate at the same level and the communication is productive.

Another game, one that is not productive is "I'm not okay, you're okay!" In this game one person does not feel good about themselves. They have learned if they bring another person, i.e. one who is okay, down to their level they subsequently feel better about themselves. It is definitely dysfunctional, but it is a game that is likely fairly common.

A bully looks at another person and decides they want to bring them down to their level. Victims are created. Victims may not even know in the beginning they have been targeted or why. Victims are not always passive individuals who are setting themselves up for bullying, as some people would believe.

A bully may target an individual who is more popular, attractive, successful, charismatic, smarter etc. than they believe they are.

This article is focusing on the on-line behaviour of a bully, also known as cyberbullying. Perhaps you will encounter them on a Facebook page as I did, or any of the numerous discussion groups that proliferate on the internet.

For whatever reason, you are chosen as their target. It might start out with their disagreement of something you have posted. Then it escalates to attacking not only your content but your credibility in posting the comments. Soon it becomes a personal attack where your personal traits and characteristics and so-called short comings are focused on.

It doesn't matter what you respond with as the bully's focus is in maintaining one-up-manship, thereby controlling you. You can tell you are dealing with a paranoid individual as they will likely respond to your post in a matter of minutes. They are at the ready, waiting for your response to be posted and then with a distant "Gottcha!" they respond caustically. "How dare you!" seems to be their battle cry.

Cyberbullies will often align themselves with influential people or organizations, where there may not be an actual connection, in order to add credence to their accusations. They will often make generalizing statements. "Everyone says that you...!" "XXX agrees with me that you..." "You always..."

So what can you do to mitigate the damage done by a cyberbully? As William Feathers is often quoted as saying "knowledge is power!" You need to regain your power from the bully and mitigate the damage they can do to you.

Something to remember is anything posted to the Internet will likely be there forever. If you are in business and trying to develop a business or personal brand via networking and/or using the Internet, it is important to think of damage control.

The following is a list of strategies you can use to regain your power from a cyberbully. They are not organized in steps, but rather initiatives that can be underway at the same time.

Social Media Discussion Groups:

If one of your posts is targeted by a bully, as hard as it will be, you need to resist the urge to respond in kind. This is what the bully wants. By responding, in their mind you justify what they wrote, and that gives them the impetus to continue and escalate their postings. It takes at least two people to argue. If you don't, it makes it more challenging for them to continue on their own.

If you are the Moderator of the group and you are under attack from a bully, I would suggest responding to them with a firm directive approach as used in the human resources field.

Provide them with an explanation of what behaviour is inappropriate, what behaviour would be appropriate and/or corrective measures you would suggest to improve the situation, a time frame for the changes to take place and finally an outline of what measures you will take if the inappropriate behaviour is not corrected. If the behaviour continues, follow through with the measures you had outlined.

It is difficult to determine how the cyberbully will respond with the above described actions. It could escalate matters. It is also difficult if not impossible to predict the future, and the past can get blurry as matters escalate.

I would recommend you create a document in your favorite word processing program to chronicle the steps you have taken in the matter and to provide evidence of the abuse directed your way.

I also recommend an inexpensive program called Snaggit from Techsmith. It allows you to take screen captures of info you want to keep. Simply highlight an area you want to capture. It loads it into the Snaggit editor where you can copy and paste into your word document.

If at anytime you feel your personal safety is at risk, notify your local police department. In my case, I sought out legal advice and was advised to take out a peace bond on the individual. This is a legal document you can present to the police should a person be within your immediate vicinity without just cause.

My local police declined following up on my complaint, saying the individual hadn't crossed over from being a nuisance to an actual threat and they were seeing an increase in this type of behaviour. Since I wasn't able to get a peace bond secured, I ensured a file was initiated at the police detachment and my details were recorded should I need to refer to them at a later date. This was all added to my personal file.

If you are the creator of the post, the bully has used as a soapbox, you are likely able to delete the entire post. This takes it away from public view. The downside of this action is should you do so, you will be unable to register a complaint with the Administrators of the specific social media. Once it is deleted, it is gone. Forever? I'm not sure about that. Make sure you make a screen shot capture before deleting the entries. We will explore how to register a complaint shortly.

Facebook:

If the post in question i.e. where you have been attacked is created by someone else, you can report it to Facebook administration by clicking on the small graphical V that appears in the top right-hand corner of the original post. It gives you the option of reporting the post or labeling it as spam. Doing so takes the post out of the Timeline and presumably Facebook will investigate it. If you are the originator of the post you only have the option of hiding your post or deleting it. Remember to take a screen capture before taking action.

Twitter:

Twitter seems to be a little more out front with how they process complaints "Users are allowed to post content, including potentially inflammatory content, provided they do not violate the Twitter Rules and Terms of Service."

"In order to investigate reports of abusive behaviors, violent threats or a breach of privacy, we need to be in contact with the actual person affected or their authorized representative. We are unable to respond to requests from uninvolved parties regarding those issues to mitigate the likelihood of false or unauthorized reports. If you are not an authorized representative but you are in contact with the individual, encourage the individual to file a report through our forms."

You can also *unfollow* a person who is harassing you on Twitter. This removes them from your timeline, but not from the Twitter stream. Their posts will remain visible on their Twitter profile homepage. Remember to take a screen capture before unfollowing them.

Linkedin:

Linkedin doesn't seem to address the issue of abusive posts other than advising that you can report inappropriate comments by flagging a group discussion.

"Open the discussion and click *Flag* to notify the group manager that an item might be inappropriate, or that it may need to be moved to the Jobs or Promotions tab.

To flag a comment in a group discussion:

Move your cursor over a comment and click *Flag as inappropriate* under a comment.

You can also contact your group owner or manager directly. The group manager decides what action (if any) will be taken.

Website or Blog:

If malicious content is being posted about you on the cyberbully's website or blog, an option is to register a complaint with their webhosting provider and/or their website developer. This information is generally available by doing a Whois domain lookup in a search engine such as Google. In my case, the website developer tried to mitigate his responsibility by saying he wasn't responsible for the content of the site, only the operating system. I left him with the idea that he may share liability should I decide to go forward with legal proceedings against the cyberbully.

Speaking of Google... it is worth your while to Google yourself every so often to see what is floating around in cyberspace about you. Simply enter your name into Google or another search engine to see what is out there. When your results are displayed, Google allows you to fine tune your search. Simply click on Search Tools and you indicate the time span that you would like displayed.

In summary, cyberbullys can make your life miserable and take your concentration away from more important issues, if you let them. To be successful at networking and self-promotion, you need to open yourself up to possibilities, and unfortunately one of those possibilities is that someone will want to take advantage of you or do harm. I hope that this article will give you strategies to regain your power should you encounter a cyberbully. Bullying in any form should not be tolerated, and we all need to do our part to reduce it. Please share this article with anyone that you feel may benefit.

IN THE NEXT CHAPTER WE LOOK SOME MISCELLANEOUS SELF-promotion and marketing tactics.

MISCELLANEOUS SELF-MARKETING & PROMOTION TACTICS

In this chapter we look some more miscellaneous self-promotion and marketing tactics.

YOUR E-MAIL SIGNATURE FILE:

A relatively easy way of promoting yourself is to develop an e-mail signature file that not only provides your contact information, it also allows you to promote yourself. They can easily be set up using Outlook, assuming you are using Outlook and a word processing program.

I've provided some examples of the ones I have used below. I believe you should have a signature file for every 'persona' you have. One of the techniques I use to self-promote is that after I have been communicating with an individual on a particular subject and under a specific signature file, I will accidently i.e. on purpose, send my message with a different signature file. This is a sneaky way of letting someone know I have other interests or services to supply. Whether it works or not, I really don't know.

Your signature file is like a small billboard that promotes you. You should make it as easy as possible for people to contact you. If you have a website, provide the URL so the reader of your e-mail can easily navigate to it. Make sure it has been hyperlinked i.e. when they click on the link it will take them to the website.

I am not currently using it on any of my signature files but many people insert a link to their Linkedin profile if they feel that there is value in doing so.

Don't forget to add a head shot photo of yourself. I expand on the subject elsewhere in this book. I often get the comment "Oh, I recognize you from your e-mail." For a shy networker this can be quite helpful. In theory, people will walk up to you and say "I know you!"

Rae Stonehouse aka Mr. Emcee
250-451-6564
rae@mremcee.com
mremcee.com
Your Okanagan Event Organizer & Master of Ceremonies of Choice
Check out our blog E=EmceeSquared
From start to finish ... we do it all!

Rae Stonehouse,
Chairman of the Board
Okanagan Valley Entrepreneurs Society (OVES)
PO Box 140-1876 Cooper Rd. Unit 138
Kelowna, B.C., V1Y 9N6
250-451-6564

rae@okanaganentrepreneurs.ca
okanaganentrepreneurs.ca

 "OVES... Driving the Entrepreneurial Spirit"

BLOW YOUR OWN HORN!

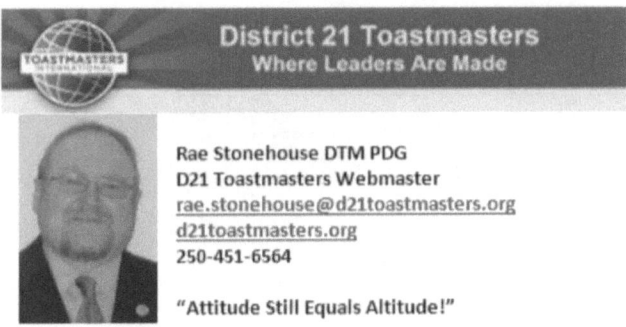

So how do we create a signature file within Outlook?

From within Outlook click on *File*. (This demonstration is using Outlook 2010.)

Next click on *Options*. Then *Mail*.

Locate and click on Signatures.

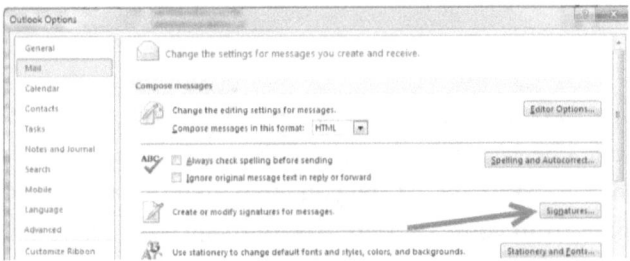

You will then open the *Signatures and Stationery* box. If this is your first time, there won't be any info displayed.

Locate and click on the *New* button. You will be prompted to *Type a name for this signature*. Use something that makes sense to you if you will be developing multiple signatures.

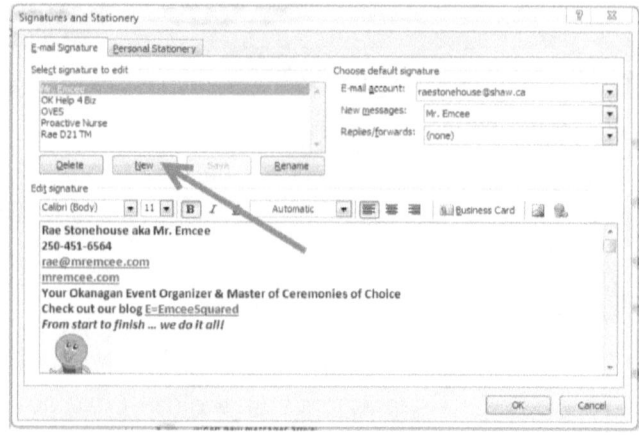

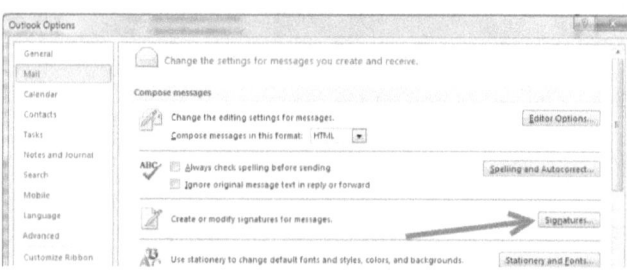

The *Edit signature* box allows you to insert your contact & promotional information. The arrow on the left in illustration above allows you to insert a photo of yourself. When you click on it, it will prompt you to add a graphic from your computer to your signature file. This step can be tedious as you might have to add your photo, save it, then open up a new message in Outlook to see if your photo is in the right scale i.e. not too small, not too large.

The second arrow allows you to add a hyperlink to any text in your message. You would highlight the text you want to be hyperlinked and click on the globe icon. You will then be prompted for the next steps.

When you have your info the way that you want it, click on *OK*, which is the same as saving. The next step would be to open up a new message in your Outlook to see how it looks.

I mentioned above that you need to ensure your photo is to scale i.e. in relation to the rest of your signature. Another consideration is how the photo is situated related to the text. Outlook doesn't do a good job of placing a photo with the accompanying text. It doesn't look like what you see in the *Edit Signature* box. The workaround is to locate the signature files Outlook saved on your hard drive and open them up in Word. You can do this by using the Search function in Microsoft Explorer, [assuming you are working on a PC] which searches your directories for files with the name you have provided. Once you locate the file, open it in Word and you can use the photo positioning features in Word to wrap the text around your photo. I always have my photo justified to the left with the text blocked to the right i.e. the text starts at the top of the graphic and works towards the bottom.

IN THE NEXT CHAPTER WE LOOK AT SOME ADDITIONAL SOCIAL MEDIA venues of value to you in self-promotion and marketing.

HOW TO NETWORK ON SOCIAL MEDIA LIKE A PRO: INTRO

In the next few chapters we look at additional social media venues that may be of value to you in self-promotion and marketing.

I mentioned in an earlier chapter that I believe Linkedin is the best social media venue for networking. While I don't believe Pinterest, Twitter and Instagram are good places to develop a business network, they can provide an opportunity to promote yourself.

This self-promotion can increase other's awareness of you and what you have to offer, which in time, could lead to developing a networking connection.

Here is a brief overview of some advantages and disadvantages of the more popular ones. My personal belief and experience is they are an incredible amount of work for limited gain.

"If you are doing your best, you will not have to worry about failure." Robert S. Hillyer

"Resolve to be a master of change rather than a victim of change." Brian Tracy

"A feeling of confidence and personal power comes from facing challenges and overcoming them." Brian Tracy

FACEBOOK

Facebook has been around for a while. If you don't use it on a regular or casual basis, I would expect you are well aware of what it is.

Whereas Linkedin can be considered your *professional* networking venue of choice, Facebook can very well be considered your *social* networking venue of choice. There is room for both.

Facebook has changed considerably over the years. It was once a good place to self-promote at no cost to you. It has developed into a 'pay to play' model in that you are strongly urged by Facebook to pay for their advertising services to promote a product or service you are behind.

You may have numerous Facebook *Followers* but that doesn't mean they will see most, if any of your posts. Facebook has instituted algorithms that send your postings to those who you have responded or interacted with you lately. Facebook desires an interactive community of happy members.

Note: Some content for this chapter and section is adapted from my book **The Power of Promotion: On-line Marketing for Toastmasters Club Growth.** While it was originally written for a Toastmasters club's perspective, the same principles apply in setting up a self-promotion/marketing venue.

When thinking of self-promotion on Facebook, you have some considerations.

Group Page vs Fan page / Open Group vs Closed Group

Facebook Pages, formerly called *'fan pages'*, enable public figures, businesses & organizations to create a public presence on Facebook. *Facebook Pages* are visible to everyone on the Internet by default. All somebody has to do is *'Like'* your page and they can follow and interact with everything that gets posted to your *Page*. Your updates will show up in their *News Feed (Timeline)*.

Facebook Groups on the other hand can be an effective way for an organization to share discussions and common interests among the members in a way that is more private than a *Facebook Page*. When you create a *Group*, you can decide whether to make it publicly available for anyone to join, require administrator approval for members to join or keep it private and by invitation only. This allows the Administrator some control in who they let in for membership. As a private group you have the option of who you admit for membership and who you don't.

As an Administrator for several Facebook Groups I tend to check out every applicant to see if they have a connection to the particular group in some way. If I don't see a connection or friends of theirs in the group, I deny their membership. There is a fad taking place right now, for lack of a better word, where individuals seem to be competing with each other to see how many groups they can join. I have personally seen several requests from individuals in a day to join a particular Facebook Group. Each of them had over a thousand groups that they were members of. As I mentioned before, unless I saw some connection with the group they were applying to join, I would deny their membership.

Similar to *Pages*, new *posts* by a *Group* are included in the *News Feeds* of its members and members can interact and share with one another from the group.

Whether you opt for a *closed*, membership-only group or a *wide-open* fan page, there is value to giving some consideration to developing *Terms of Reference* for the group. These terms in essence outline what is *appropriate* conduct and what is *inappropriate* conduct. It also allows the *Administrator* to state what the consequences of misbehaviour would be. This is likely more enforceable within a *Facebook Group* than it would be in a *Page*.

While you want to engage your fans with discussion i.e. back-and-forth discussion, you need to be aware of the risk of doing so. Even though as Toastmasters we like to think that we are a more enlightened and respectful group, there will always be individuals who don't share our values. An old on-line term for them is 'trolls' more commonly known now as *cyberbullies*.

A cyberbully will use your Facebook discussion/timeline to forward *their* agenda. It may be to make themselves look more important than they really are or perhaps they like using a public forum to create a shock reaction. As the Administrator of the group, you need to be vigilant in ensuring that this behaviour doesn't start in the first place and taking proactive action if it does. I'll talk some more about this a little later.

I talked about Cyberbullies in a previous chapter.

Some organizations have tried to maintain control of the comments posted on their *Facebook Pages* by not allowing the public i.e. fans/followers to post to their *Timeline*. While this action may help them in the short-term I personally feel that by restricting input, they are also restricting dialogue. I don't care much for *Facebook Pages* that are strictly promoting to me or feeding me their info without allowing me to respond in kind.

I'm not going to expand upon how to set up and manage your Facebook presence at this point as it could easily fill another publication. Facebook itself offers plenty of resource files to do so.

In an upcoming chapter on using Twitter to self-promote, I make comment about not linking your Twitter account to your Facebook account to post all your tweets. However, the opposite connecting your Facebook account to your Twitter account is a good idea.

How to Link Your Facebook Page and Content to other Social Media

I've mentioned the value in connecting your *Facebook Page* and your *Twitter* account. If you haven't already, create a *Twitter* profile and then you can set it up so your *Facebook* posts automatically post to Twitter. We explore how to set up Twitter account later on in this book.

Here's how to set it up:

1. Login to *Facebook*

2. Open a second browser tab

3. Login to your *Twitter* profile

Click your profile icon. It's in the top-right side of the Twitter page, just left of the *Tweet* button...

Click *Settings* and *Privacy*. This option is near the bottom of the drop-down menu.

Click the Apps tab. You'll find it on the left side of the page.

Click Connect to Facebook.

Log into Facebook if you aren't already.

Click OK.

Having said I wasn't going to dive into showing you how to set up your Facebook page or group, there are some areas I do want to expand upon, starting with your *About* section.

The following content assumes you have set your Facebook up as a business.

When you click on *About*, you will be taken to the *Page Info* section which contains a list of headings for you to add details.

Category: The Company, Organization, or Institution category is best if customers don't frequent your physical location, or if you hold events at varying places.

A *Local Business* category is best if your agency deals with any locally owned business in your area. It will optimize the search results for those business owners and managers in your area looking for your marketing expertise.

Name: This should be fairly obvious as to what you would enter here, but then again, maybe it isn't. Under this category you would enter the name of your business, not your personal name.

Facebook Web Address: This seems a little redundant to me as the url of your Facebook Page would be displaying in your browser, however it provides an additional mentioning of your business' Facebook Page web address.

Start Date: This would be the start date of your business, not the date you started the Facebook Page. If your business has been around for a while it gives you some bragging rights.

Address: You have at least two choices as to what you can add here, either the address of your bricks and mortar business or the designated mailing address of your business if you don't have a physical property.

Hours: Insert the hours your business is open or when you are available to be contacted.

Short Description: You can show a brief description of approximately 155 characters that displays below the Cover Image and the Profile Image at the top of your Page. This is great space to outline a concise statement about your business and list your website URL.

Tip: Keep it short and sweet, and add your website URL, hyperlinked.

Otherwise, visitors have to click on *About*, and hunt for your website URL there. The short description is the best way to add an up front and clearly visible path to your website.

Impressum: Short version, you don't need to worry about this section. Slightly longer version... this is an optional field. In certain countries such as Austria, Germany & Switzerland businesses may be required by law to include a statement of ownership on their web presence. There is a limitation of 2000 characters.

Company Overview: This is another opportunity for you to add some promotional content not covered in your *Short* or *Long Description*.

Long Description: This area gives you lots of room for promotional copy or a longer version of what your business is all about. You can add over 30000 characters in this section. If you have a dedicated website for your business, you may want to create promotional copy designed to lure the visitor to your website.

The intent would be the copy on the website would be crafted to encourage a visitor to your site to contact you. Conversely, if you don't have a personal or business website, you may want to take advantage of this space to add promotional copy with the same aim in mind i.e. encouraging them to visit your business or to contact you.

It's a fact of life that some visitors to your Facebook Page won't take the extra step to visit your website. Don't be afraid to duplicate the promotional copy from your website in this area.

One benefit of utilizing this category is that Google indexes all the information posted. This can help with visibility in search engine results.

The mission of this chapter is to provide you with tips & techniques to self-promote by using Facebook. The term "using" implies that there is some action required on your part to make traffic happen. I believe a big mistake many *Fan Page* owners make is that they post their content, then leave it alone. The action required is that your page needs fresh content on a regular basis. If a visitor to your page sees the same content every time that they visit, why should they visit again? Odds are that they won't!

To be an effective marketing tool your club *Facebook Page* needs to be the following: informational, entertaining, educational, thought-provoking, engaging, interactive, timely and addictive. Okay, the addictive might seem a little odd but you want people to be compelled to see what you are posting on your site and to share on their own Timeline.

Content can be created from within your business, from other similar business' Facebook Pages, and/or their websites. There are many sources of shareable on-line content.

From Your Own Computer & Imagination:

Turn motivational quotes into graphics. Be sure to add an appropriate comment above the graphic, e.g., why is this graphic important. Think tweeting! I'll be explaining this a little later, but you should be considering linking your Facebook Fan Page with a Twitter account.

Each of these on-line social venues likely reach different audiences. If your Facebook and Twitter account are linked and you post a graphic to your Facebook, no information, other than the link to the graphic will show on the Twitter feed. However, if you post some opening commentary, it will post on Twitter.

Post useful/interesting articles from other on-line sources. Content should be related to your business or field of interest/expertise.

A good source of fresh content I use regularly is Google Alerts.

Google Alerts: https://www.google.ca/alerts Alerts allow you to monitor the web for any new articles on any subject you are interested in and have it sent to you on a daily basis as an e-mail. You simply insert your keyword and create an Alert. You can have multiple alerts based on your keywords. Google will create a list of articles/websites it notices on the web and then send them to you. Many of the offerings are not relevant, but there can be gems hidden within the listings.

After clicking on the hyperlink within the listing, copy the url of the article and the title and paste them into your Timeline.

Posting fresh content is a great way to build a loyal following and is one step closer to converting a Facebook fan to a personal or business connection. Keep in mind some of your fans may live anywhere in the world and may be following you because of the interesting content you are posting.

While posting fresh, thought-provoking content is integral to the effectiveness of your Facebook Page, it plays only one part of the formula.

Another important part, and one that is also time consuming, is that of keeping the conversation going. You as the Administrator need to add comments or pose questions to posts on a regular basis.

As an Administrator you need to acknowledge Likes or Comments in a timely manner. People tend to check on their posts regularly to see if there are any feedback/comments. An acknowledgment can be as simple as saying thank-you or more in-depth by expanding upon the original post/comment or taking it in a different direction.

Question: "How often should I post to my Facebook Page?"

Answer: It depends on several factors. If you as the Administrator are the only one posting to the *Timeline*, likely two to four posts a day is adequate. If you only have a small group of followers, any more than four posts a day may not be a good investment of your time.

On the other hand, if your following is fairly large and members are actively participating by posting their own posts and/or Liking & Sharing from the Timeline, it might be worth your while to increase the amount of posts you publish to the Timeline as the Administrator. Breaking the day into sections may help to develop a publishing schedule e.g., early morning 8 am, late morning 11ish, early afternoon 1:30, late afternoon 4:30 and mid evening 8:30 pm.

I liken developing and growing a Facebook Page to growing a sour dough culture. To make sour dough 'grow' you need to add milk and flour on a regular basis. If you continue to do so, you can have a sour dough culture that can last decades.

I've heard marketing claims of sour dough starter being available for purchase that dates back to the gold rush days, i.e. the late 1800s in North America. If you don't take care of the culture, i.e. store it at the proper temperature, use it occasionally and feed it regularly, it will eventually die out.

Your Facebook Page has many similarities to growing a sour dough culture. You need to work at it to get it growing. You have to nourish it by adding interesting content to your Timeline, and you have to be expanding it by enticing new 'friends' to follow you.

If you only feed it periodically with new content or stop completely, your followers... won't be following you anymore.

How to Add Graphics to Your Posts

Graphics grab our attention. They create a curiosity in us to read the accompanying text, more so than the same text would if it was posted without the graphic.

It is often said that a picture is worth a thousand words. If the rest of that particular saying needs to be completed perhaps it should be the picture/graphic also has to be self-explanatory. It shouldn't take a thousand words or so to explain what the picture is about.

Social media platforms such as Facebook, readily lend themselves to being very visual. As I mentioned above, we are more likely to read the message accompanied with a graphic than we are to pass it by.

In writing the above passage I started to challenge the thought behind the writing. We accept the fact visuals grab our attention. I think you will agree with me? But is there any science behind it? Why do we accept as fact pictures do grab our attention? As I do with many other questions I have, I consulted with the world-acknowledged expert of everything... Mr. Google. I found an interesting article entitled The Power of Visual Communication by Mike Parkinson.

Mr. Parkinson provides the following: "What we see has a profound effect on what we do, how we feel, and who we are. Through experience and experimentation, we continually increase our understanding of the visual world and how we are influenced by it."

"Psychologist Albert Mehrabian demonstrated that 93% of communication is nonverbal. Studies find that the human brain deciphers image elements simultaneously, while language is decoded in a linear, sequential manner taking more time to process. Our minds react differently to visual stimuli."

He also adds "So visuals are processed 60,000 times faster than text, graphics quickly affect our emotions, and our emotions greatly affect our decision-making."

Utilizing graphics in your Facebook Posts can be quite easy or a bit challenging at times.

If you are sharing a post you have seen on another group's or an individual's *Timeline*, it can be a simple matter of clicking on the *Share* button assuming they are allowing shares. Facebook will load the graphic that has already been attached to the post and upload it to the *Timeline* you are sharing it on.

For those graphics that don't seem to be shareable, an inexpensive screen capture program like Snaggit can save the graphic to your computer where you can then share it.

Let's take a look at a couple different scenarios where you would be adding a graphic to a message and the challenges and solutions that accompany it.

One: The graphic is located on your computer.

You can easily create your own graphics using graphics software. I use two inexpensive but powerful programs for my websites and publications. Snagit by Techsmith is a screen capture program that has photo editing capabilities.

Xara Designer Pro is an affordable alternative to Adobe Photoshop. It has a fairly steep learning curve, however the company provides lots of video tutorials to help you in your projects. You can get a good deal from them on-line for existing products when they introduce an upgrade to the marketplace.

I would suggest you create directories on your hard drive labeled *Facebook Page*, then a sub directory called *Graphics*. Upload any graphics you collect or create to the *Graphics* subfolder. This puts all of your graphics in one easy to locate spot.

I have a directory called Social Media where I collect graphics in the following subdirectories: Elders, Facebook, Gifs, Jobs Photos, Linkedin, Networking, Random Photos, Reading Related, Toastmasters and Twitter. I have a few Facebook pages and groups.

I would offer a cautionary note at this point about ownership and usage of graphics that are readily found on the Internet. Just because it is on-line and somebody else has used it, doesn't mean you can too. You do so at your own risk.

There are stories of authors and website developers receiving official legal correspondence advising them they are in copyright infringement and owe the graphic creator $10000, immediately.

If you are the creator of the graphic or artistic work, you are considered the author and the copyright owner. With the development of inexpensive graphic artistry software, more and more people are doing so. If you incorporate other people's work into your own work, a derivative product, you may once again be in violation of someone's copyright.

Having issued that caution, graphics are readily available on the Internet for download. Some are expensive, many are relatively inexpensive and many are available for free. Just do a Google search for *'free graphics'* and you will be presented with a large selection. With research you should be able to find a graphic on virtually any topic.

I am fond of Flickr, particularly the Creative Commons. I search for graphics where the author has granted permission to use the photo how I please and all I have to do is provide credit to them in the body of my creative work, whether it be an article, blog post or website.

For other times when I have needed a specific photo to make my message I am quite willing to pay a fair price for the product.

So, to upload a graphic stored on your computer, locate the following on your *Timeline* and click on the *Photo/Video* link.

Two: The graphic is located on an article or blog post that you want to feature on your Timeline.

Facebook can be finicky and frustrating when you try to upload an article or it can be amazingly simple.

This process is a little different from the previous one where we were uploading a graphic from our computer. In this case the graphic is located somewhere else, that we don't have any control over. Taking a look at our *Timeline* again you insert the url (web address) of the webpage that you want to feature where it says "What have you been up to?"

Your url will be visible in the *Timeline* box and Facebook will pull the graphic from the website... maybe!

If there are multiple graphics on the website you are drawing from, Facebook can sometimes have difficulty choosing which photo is the one to grab. It may give you a selection of 2 to 5 choose from. If one of them is the one that you want, simply click on it and it will be loaded.

Now what happens if the selection of graphics Facebook offers doesn't include the one you want, or doesn't offer any choices i.e. no graphic, what do you next?

The solution is relatively easy but does take time. As I write this, I realized it is relatively easy to me because I have done it hundreds of times and I have the software to do so. The first step is you need to capture the graphic from the website by either using screen capture software or by clicking on the graphic with your left mouse button and then clicking your right mouse button (assuming you are right handed) and clicking on *Save Image As...*

You will be prompted as to where you want to save your image. The *Graphics* folder I mentioned above is a good location. You would then upload your graphic in the same method I mentioned earlier.

This should be easy enough but you may find your graphic is too large or too small to be posted and doesn't display very well. This means you would have to edit your graphic to get it to fit. It can be very much trial and error with creating posts, adding the graphic, if it fits... fine... if not delete the post, edit the graphic, insert the graphic to the *Timeline*, over and over until it fits.

While adding graphics to your post can exponentially increase the odds, your message will be posted, you still need to add some text to your post.

Adding Video to Facebook:

A statistic from 2017 said over 8 billion videos or 100 million hours of videos are watched on Facebook every day. We can only assume that statistic has grown since then.

Video is very popular on-line, especially with our modern high-speed Internet connections.

Instead of diving into the how to of maximizing your Facebook video, I'll offer this on-line resource for you to check out.

17 Ways to Get More Views, Engagement, and Shares for Your Facebook Videos:

https://buffer.com/library/facebook-video#square-videos

Here is a quick view of their list. You can read the details at the link above.

- Create square videos

- Catch people's attention within the first 3 seconds
- Add captions to your videos
- Suggest viewers tap for sound
- Focus on one key point
- Upload your videos natively (via Buffer!)
- Craft a descriptive title
- Create a Facebook-specific copy
- Give a preview of the video in your copy
- Add a call-to-action
- Tag other pages
- Choose preferred audience for your videos
- Use insights to understand video performance
- Go live
- Feature a video on your Page
- Boost with Facebook ads
- Embed Facebook videos on blog posts

Many people use Facebook to link to videos that are already uploaded to YouTube, both theirs and others. Facebook prefers you to upload directly to them rather than using a YouTube link.

Here are some best practices from Facebook on using video:

Capture attention quickly

Using colors, themes and imagery that evoke your brand at the start of your video can help people connect the video and your brand quickly. Consider starting your video with lifestyle and product shots, recognizable spokespeople, action scenes or a vivid background to spark interest.

Design for sound off

Because most videos in mobile feed are viewed without sound, it's important to convey your message visually. Showing captions, logos and products can help communicate your message, even in silence.

Frame your visual story

Producing video for a small screen requires consideration of dimension and scale. Play with zoom, crop and overall visual composition to make sure that your story is told well on a small screen.

Play around and learn what works

There's no universal solution to building brands or driving actions with mobile video, so keep experimenting, testing and iterating to learn what works for your brand and audience.

Video upload specs

We support almost all types of video files, but recommend using the MP4 format.

Resolution should be 1080p or less.

We support file sizes up to 10 GB; there may be longer upload times associated with larger files on slower Internet connections.

Videos must be less than 240 minutes long. The longer your video is, the larger its file size will be. This may affect the quality of the video, and the time it takes to upload.

We also recommend Stereo AAC audio compression with 128 kbps or more.

In an upcoming chapter we talk about cross-promoting your videos between Facebook and YouTube.

IN THE NEXT CHAPTER WE LOOK AT OPTIMIZING FACEBOOK FOR search engines to help you be visible.

SEARCH ENGINE OPTIMIZATION FOR FACEBOOK

The following is a list of suggestions gleaned from the Internet to optimize your *Facebook Page* for search engines. The idea is to make your *Page* more attractive, so it is placed higher in the search engine results. You want to be as high in the rankings as possible.

Research has shown that many on-line viewers only check out the first page or two on the subject they are interested in, before moving on. You want your *Facebook Page* to be placed in the top of the first page.

If you are using your *Facebook Page* as a way to attract guests to your Toastmaster's club or other cause you have and there are others in your geographical area/market, it is worth your while to take a few extra steps to ensure the search engines actually notice you, let alone place you high in the standings.

The quickest way to see if your *Facebook Page* has been indexed by a particular search engine is to copy and paste the *Facebook* url into your browser's *Search* box. If it has been indexed, it should come up at the top of the listings provided.

Note: Search engines such as Google change their algorithms i.e. the computer program used to index sites, regularly... so what works today, may not work tomorrow.

- **Choose the best name for your Facebook Page–and don't change it.**

Use your Toastmaster's club's real name as the name of your page, rather than a promotional-based one e.g., *Kelowna Flying Solo Toastmasters* vs *"The Best Toastmasters Club in Kelowna... Flying Solo Toastmasters."* It may be true... but Google would penalize you if you did so.

And once you pick your *Page's* name, don't change it. Facebook uses your *Page* name in the title of the *Page*, and since Google dings (punishes) pages when their titles change, modifying your *Facebook Page's* name will cost you SEO points.

If your Toastmasters club name doesn't actually have the word 'Toastmasters' as part of it, you should add it to your **Facebook Page** name for better recognition and search engine indexing.

- **Select the best URL (Facebook username) for your Facebook Page.**

By default, your *Facebook Page* will get a randomly assigned number and URL, like facebook.com/pages/yourbusiness/123456789. Facebook allows you to create a *vanity url* for your page. Facebook calls it a *"username"*. This is one of the most important actions you can take to increase your SEO opportunities to date.

When you choose a Facebook username for your *Page,* your *Page's* URL becomes *www.facebook.com/YourUsernameHere*. Usernames can be selected at www.facebook.com/username.

Choosing a username is totally optional, but it adds an extra level of professionalism and gives you a shorter, more memorable web address for your business page. Don't hesitate -- you want to ensure that you get your business name before someone else does!

- **Use the "About" text box to place keyword-dense prose near the top of your Page.**

We've already discussed maximizing your *About* box in a previous chapter. This section looks at it from an SEO perspective.

One important SEO strategy that should be employed on your *Facebook Page* whenever feasible is placing keyword-dense prose as close to the top of the *Page* as possible.

Because Facebook limits where *Page* owners can place large chunks of text on the default Wall tab of Facebook Pages, the "About" box actually represents the highest place in the CSS structure of the page to add custom text.

In order to add text to your Page's "*About*" area, click the "*About*" box underneath your Page's profile picture. You will be taken to your *About* page for editing where you can insert promotional copy under the categories of: *Short Description, Company Overview, Long Description and General Information.*

Each section has its own limitations as to how much content you can add. The *Long Description* is an excellent place to add urls to your club website or to other web locations you may want to draw traffic to.

Facebook previously had an "*Info*" tab that allowed you to include more important keywords, text and high priority links on your page. Now this *info i*s included in the *About* page.

It's important to fill out these fields, because they provide the opportunity to include keywords, prose, and links that will increase the content score of your *Facebook Page* for many types of Google searches. For example:

- **Address** is an important field for *local searches*.
- **Company Overview, Mission, Products** are important fields for *product searches*.
- **Websites** is a valuable opportunity to add direct links to your own websites or other relevant sites that you want to promote.

- **Be sure to include your phone number and address.**

  - As surprising as it sounds, there are a lot of businesses out there that don't include this type of info on their fan page. But remember, indexing your brand for local search results is crucial to growing your *Facebook fan page.*
  - In addition, Google places higher importance on pages with specific information like your business's phone number and address. So, pages that include this type of data can effectively increase your brand's overall SEO.

The specific fields present will vary according to the category you choose for your *Page* when you create it (business, brand, or public figure), so choose the category that best fits your needs.

- **Post direct links to your website (or other relevant sites) in your Page's Timeline.**

When you include the raw URL in the text of the status update itself, *Facebook* auto-links the text directly to the URL. While you can't control the anchor text of the link (it is always just the URL itself), the link does go directly to the destination page – and not through a Facebook.com URL that adds the Facebook menu bar at the top when you click through to the destination page.

Once *Facebook* has pulled the content in from where you are linking to, it isn't important to keep the actual URL when it comes to SEO purposes, since your post will serve as the metadata for the link you shared. Deleting the full URL also helps out your viral growth rate by making your post a little prettier and share-friendly.

- **Add photos with captions & events with descriptions.**

It almost goes without saying, but it's important to always be sharing interesting content on your *Facebook Page*, and always using all available descriptive fields on each type of content shared.

When posting photos, use verbose and keyword-dense descriptions. When posting events, take the extra minute to include text and keywords in the event description field that you want to rank for.

Facebook makes all the content shared on *Facebook Pages* indexable by search engines, so use the tools Facebook provides to your full advantage.

- **Get more inbound links to your Facebook Page from the web by posting links to your Page on all your websites.**

Just as a variety of inbound links from authoritative websites help boost Page Rank for traditional websites, getting more inbound links to your *Facebook Page* will boost its PageRank and visibility as well. Think of links as 'votes.' The more votes you get, the more popular you are.

There are two ways to use links to your advantage. The first way is to use links to build up your fan base. More fans will help increase the popularity of your fan page.

The second way is to use external links that point to your fan page. Make sure you have links on your site or blog that promote your fan page. Promote this to any of your friends or partners and have them link there as well.

You can do this with text links, but Facebook has also created a *"Find Us On Facebook"* badge, which it encourages **Page** owners to use. More info on creating Facebook badges can be found at https://www.facebook.com/badges/

If you are the website administrator for your club website, it can be a simple matter of adding one of the plethora of *"Find Us"* icons, as illustrated below, into your website with a link to your Toastmaster Club's *Facebook Page.*

- **Get more intra-Facebook inbound links by getting more Facebook fans.**

The more inbound links to your page, the more authoritative your page is according to Google, and you will be ranked higher. That is why it is very important to bloggers when they have their content linked to from other websites, blogs, etc.

This same principle applies to your *Facebook Fan Page*. So, where it is appropriate, include a link to your fan page from your other digital channels, like your website, blog, and Twitter profile.

In addition, because Facebook places links to *Facebook Pages* on the default version of Facebook users' profile pages which are visible to search engines, the more fans you get, the more links you'll have to your *Page* within Facebook. For *Pages* with thousands (or even millions) of fans, the number of links can really add up.

- **Strengthen intra-Facebook reciprocal linking by getting fans to comment and like content in your stream.**

When fans comment or like content in your *Facebook Page's* stream, Facebook links their name back to their Facebook profile page. As a result, when the profile stubs of those fans who have posted comments and likes on your *Page* are indexed, Google will see more reciprocal links between your *Page* and your *Page's* fans (in a way that grows organically over time), which it will see as a stronger bond. This creates a virtuous cycle of improved link weight from the indexed profile page stubs to your *Page*, and vice versa.

Author's Note: While this previous tip seems to be logical, I have been unable to validate it myself.

- **Optimize Facebook fan page status updates.**

When posting updates to your *Facebook Timeline*, remember that the first 18 characters of a Facebook post serve as the meta description. So, take advantage of the option when Facebook prompts you to "Write something..." since that text will be considered the SEO title for that update. Including direct links to your Toastmaster's club website in your updates is also a good practice to follow.

Quick Tip: Just like your fan *Page's* name, Google places a higher importance on the first word of your update, so you may want to consider making that a keyword.

In the next chapter, we look at using Twitter for self-promotion.

> "Resolve to be a master of change rather than a victim of change." Brian Tracy
>
> "A feeling of confidence and personal power comes from facing challenges and overcoming them." Brian Tracy
>
> "Concentrate on one thing, the most important thing, and stay with it until it's complete." Brian Tracy

TWITTER

The content for this chapter is adapted from my book **The Power of Promotion: On-line Marketing for Toastmasters Club Growth**. While it was originally written for a Toastmasters club's perspective, the same principles apply in setting it up as a self-promotion/marketing tool.

Wikipedia described Twitter as follows: "Twitter is an on-line social networking service that enables users to send and read short 280-character messages called *"tweets"*.

Registered users can read and post *tweets*, but unregistered users can only read them. Users access Twitter through the website interface, SMS, or mobile device app.

WikiHow to do anything described Twitter in the following manner "could be called a 'real time social networking' site, a place for sharing information as it happens, and for connecting with others in real time, often resulting in lasting friendships and contacts."

Advantages:

- It is relatively easy to set up a Twitter account to market

BLOW YOUR OWN HORN!

yourself or your cause.
- It is easy for a Twitter member to follow you and *"Favorite"* & *"Share"* your tweets.
- Twitter profiles are indexed by most search engines, actual posts/content by some.
- Some search engines index individual *tweets*.
- Integrates well with Facebook, YouTube and your website.
- Fresh content is relatively easy to create.
- Easy to create a tweet campaign [bulk tweeting].
- A sizeable *Followers* amount indicates social proof. Social proof is where people believe if a large amount of others are following you... you must be worthwhile following

Disadvantages/Considerations:

- A person needs to be a member of Twitter to follow you and communicate with you i.e. DM (Direct Message).
- *Follows* are more likely to be worldwide, rather than local.
- Your number of *followers* doesn't mean all of those Twitter members actually follow you or care about what you post.
- It takes time to create fresh content [actually a lot of time!].
- You have to post frequently so you stand out in the crowd of other Twitter profiles.
- It takes considerable time and effort to create a list of followers.
- Member to member communication can be stilted. If you don't check regularly, you could miss conversations.
- You only have 280 characters for your post, including your link i.e. url.
- Personal conversations are taking place on Twitter that should be conducted in person.

Note: The limit is now 280 characters, the most common length of a *tweet i*s 33 characters. Historically, only 9% of *tweets* hit Twitter's 140-character limit, now it's 1%.

. . .

How to Create Your Twitter Account

The first step is sign up with Twitter.

To create an account on the web:

1. Go to http://twitter.com and find the sign up box, or go directly to https://twitter.com/signup.
2. Enter your *full name, phone number, and a password*.
3. Click *Sign up for Twitter*.
4. In order to verify your phone number, they will send you an SMS text message with a code. Enter the verification code in the box provided.
5. Once you've clicked *Sign up for Twitter,* you can select a *username* (usernames are unique identifiers on *Twitter*) -- type your own or choose one they've suggested. They'll tell you if the username you want is available.
6. Double-check your name, phone number, password, and username.
7. Click *Create my account*. You may be asked to complete a Captcha to let them know that you're human.

Note: if you'd like to sign up with Twitter using an email address, you can do so via the *"Use email instead"* link at the bottom of the sign up page.

Source: https://support.twitter.com/articles/100990#

Tips for picking a username:

Your *username* is the name your followers use when sending @replies, mentions, and direct messages.

It will also form the URL of your Twitter profile page. They will provide a few available suggestions when you sign up, but feel free to choose your own.

Please note: You can change your *username* in your account settings at any time, as long as the new username is not already in use.

Usernames must be fewer than 15 characters in length and cannot contain "admin" or "Twitter", in order to avoid brand confusion.

[Author's Comments]

<u>Note:</u> The Twitter username you choose should be consistent and recognizable as your name. With only 15 characters available, you may have to be creative in developing a name that fits your personality and another hasn't taken.

Setting Up Your Twitter Profile

One of the first exposures to your Twitter profile a visitor would encounter is the *Header*. Very much the same as the *Header* in *Facebook* it allows you to promote your brand, a sense of what your group is all about, or perhaps make a statement of significance to you.

When you first start out you will have a blank screen with an *Edit Profile* button available.

Creating Your Twitter Profile Header:

If this a new profile, clicking on the *Edit Profile* button will allow you to *Change your header photo*. Clicking on *Change your header photo* will give you the option of uploading your photo for the first time or removing it and uploading another.

Profile Header: 1500px by 500px. Panoramas work well. While 1500px x 500px is the recommended size, if you don't want Twitter to resize the image, you can get away with 1263px x 421px. But even when it's not being resized, it'll still get crunched with heavy JPG compression.

Source: http://havecamerawilltravel.com/photographer/twitter-layout-profile-image-sizes

<u>Note:</u> As in uploading a header photo for Facebook you may need to try several different sizes or even different graphics to find something that appeals to you.

Twitter Profile Picture:

400px by 400px is the recommended size. It's displayed as a square image with rounded corners (the corners are applied automatically) and a thin white border. If you upload an image that isn't a square, you're given the option to reposition or zoom in when you upload.

Note: Once again, your *Profile Picture* is one of the first things a visitor to your profile page or a *Follower* would encounter and it should be consistent with your personal branding.

Adding text and other elements to your Twitter Profile can be challenging. I have tended to avoid it in various profiles.

For further advice on adding Text, Logos, Watermarks on Twitter Profile Images I would recommend going to http://havecamerawilltravel.com/photographer/twitter-layout-profile-image-sizes for a better description than I can provide.

In addition to adding a graphic for your *Header & Profile Picture* you can add *promotional text* to your *Bio*. You are limited to 160 characters. Your *Twitter Bio* needs to be "punchy and to the point!" to attract a potential follower's attention.

Step by Step Use of Twitter:

This next section is courtesy of *WikiHow* and is provided for your convenience as an easier method of providing a quick tutorial on how to use Twitter to promote your Toastmaster's club.

The content reflects the views of the original submitters, not necessarily the author of this book. Links have been provided for your convenience. Additional graphics that help illustrate the particular step or point being made can be viewed on their website. Some hyperlinks are available to provide you with additional information from their site. Any additional comments or something I would like to draw your attention to will be identified as **[Author's Comments]** and as such should not be considered part of **WikiHow's** content.

1) Learn the Twitter lingo and use it appropriately.

Tweet - a Twitter single update of 280 or fewer characters, which can include @Mentions to other users, hashtags, external links, or simply regular text.

Retweet or "RT" - taking a tweet from one user and posting it yourself, automatically crediting the source, so all of your followers can see the *tweet*. The original retweeting style would take a tweet and re-post it via your own account in the following format: 'RT @(username of person who originally tweeted the *tweet* you're retweeting): (contents of tweet)'. The current system does away with this format, and instead directly re-posts the tweet, crediting the origin underneath. For example, 'retweeted from @username'.

TweetUps - Using Twitter to meet with other Twitter folks.

Trending Topics (TTs) – "Trending Topics" lists a range of subjects which many users across Twitter are talking about simultaneously.

When Twitter first got started, "Trending Topics" were those which were most popular during the span of the entire previous week. But new, more advanced algorithms have now made it easier to detect recent trends, and cite the very latest most-talked-about subjects.

These days, the "Trending Topics" list contains things that thousands of people across the whole of Twitter are discussing at any one time. When you click on a Trending Topic in the list, it will bring up a range of tweets, mentioning each matter of interest, and for each Trending Topic there will be up to three 'Top Tweets' highlighted--Those are the *tweets* in each topic which have been retweeted more than 150 times. You can view a list of trends in your area in the right-hand column of the homepage.

Lists - Users can organize the people they follow into lists of businesses or personalities which are related in some way. For example, a user could list all of the NPOs (Not for Profit Organizations) and charities they follow into a single list, for easy reference.

Promoted Tweets - A single trending topic which a company or organization can pay to 'trend', as to gain attention and traffic from Twitter users worldwide.

Source: http://www.wikihow.com/Use-Twitter

2) Tweet. If you want to let your *Followers* know what you are doing, type it into the 'What's happening?' text box and then click on the *'Tweet'* button. Note that tweets are limited to 280 or fewer characters; otherwise, the *"Tweet"* button will go into a minus.

As you type, a countdown is offered to help you keep track of the character count of your *tweets*. The allowed characters are in gray, then the last 10 go red, and then a red minus symbol appears when you are past the zero (0) indicator.

Source: http://www.wikihow.com/Use-Twitter

3) Use hashtags. Prefacing a word with a '#' will create a hashtag. A hashtag makes a certain word easily searchable.

- Some Trending topics will include hashtags, thus making it easier for users to tap into a Twitter-wide conversation regarding a single matter of interest.
- A prime example of the usage of hashtags can be seen with Major League Baseball, which uses team-name hashtags (#Mets, for example) to pull together lists of in-game *tweets*, which they display on their website.

Source: http://www.wikihow.com/Use-Twitter

4) Gather Followers. Your Twitter can be as intimate or as big as you choose. If your goal is to gather lots of followers, though, be sure to keep your posts interesting and relevant. You shouldn't underestimate the power of following others, either—often times if you follow someone they'll follow you back.

Finally, give your favorite followers shout outs occasionally. This could be through direct tweets, blogs, or a simple #FF (#FollowFriday) mechanism. This is where you tweet a short list of your key followers who you think would be good for others to follow and include the hashtag #FF, they are generally sent out at the end of the week hence the name.

This will often be reciprocated, meaning your name gets circulated. However, #FollowFridays are going out of fashion and many commentators question their worth due to their spam-like nature. A simple RT (re-tweet) can be a very effective way of attracting followers. Re-tweets are a real time affirmation of someone else's statement and is often rewarded with a follow.

Source: http://www.wikihow.com/Use-Twitter

[Author's Comments]

The more *Followers* you have, the more likely your content or promotional material will be viewed. As mentioned in the *Disadvantages* section above, your number of *Followers* doesn't necessarily mean people are actually reading your posts.

As soon as you create your Twitter account and go live, you will seem to automatically get *Followers*. I'm not sure how this happens. Perhaps they have software programs that allow them to automatically *follow* someone based on specific parameters they have inputted.

While it is good to have some *Followers* to start with, they are not necessarily interested in you.

In originally writing this section I took my own advice and started *Following* a couple dozen Toastmasters/public speaking related *Twitter* profiles to add to my club's *Following* from this club's profile. Moments after I did this, notifications of people *Following* me back started to appear in my Outlook e-mail Inbox.

The next step is to click on any of the profiles that you have *Followed* and see who they are *Following*. Just repeat the same process, clicking on any profile of interest to rapidly increase your list of who you are *Following*.

While this method can rapidly increase the number that you are *Following*, equally important is that you have to get people to Follow you. Here is where something called the '*Law of Reciprocity*' comes into play. Basically, it means if you do something for someone else, they will feel obligated to do something in return for you. If you *Follow* them, they will likely feel obligated to *Follow* you.

Many will *Follow* you automatically, without checking your profile to see who you are. Others will actively check out your profile to see who and what you are all about before deciding whether to *Follow* you or not. Many may decide to *Follow* you based on the quality of your Tweets. If it doesn't resonate with them in some manner, they may not *Follow* you.

As I have multiple Twitter profiles I tend to be particular within each profile as to who I *follow* and who I don't. For me, there has to be some connection to my profile and what I am trying to promote. In our mission to promote Toastmasters via Twitter we can target market anyone with interests in Toastmasters, public speaking, leadership, networking etc.

It is also important to keep in mind that the ratio of *Followers vs Following* has to stay fairly close. Twitter has a formula they keep secret as to what ratio they accept. If they see you have rapidly increased the number of Twitter profiles you are *Following* and your own *Followers* hasn't grown at the same rate, they may penalize you by stopping your ability to *Follow* anyone else.

Once your ratio of *Followers vs Following* gets back within their parameters you will be able to continue to grow your list of *Followers*. Don't get too excited about this. I have had this happen on a few occasions. You just have to sit back and allow your *Followers* to catch up to your *Following*. If you attempt to *Follow* someone at this point and it works, then your restriction has been lifted. You are free to build your *Following* list until Twitter stops you again. There is nothing personal here, it is merely a software program doing it automatically.

5) Check the replies from your followers that are directed at you. Click '@Mentions' to see if there are any replies to any of your 'tweets'. When tweeting, using '@' followed by a username (with no spaces) in your tweet will send a mention to the user you choose. For example, '@username' will send a mention to 'username', and the entire tweet will show up in his '@mentions' section.

Source: http://www.wikihow.com/Use-Twitter

[Author's Comments]

Twitter is intended to be an interactive social media platform. You build on-line friends and connections by directly communicating with your *Followers*. Most of my Twitter activity is promotional in nature. I find it can be very easy to get caught up with other matters and not notice there has been a communication directed to me or about me until sometime later. That tends to dilute the effect.

6) Decide your own style and times for tweeting. Twitter, like many social media applications, can become addicting and time-sucking. Make a decision early on about how much time you will devote to it and about how big your 'tribe' of followers will be. Avoid worrying about getting heaps of followers; that's competitive rather than relating and it will end up wearing you out. Instead, focus on quality connections and information-sharing and don't get too upset when someone unfollows you; it happens and you can't change it. If you feel Twitter is overwhelming at any time, simply take a break from it and come back later, refreshed.

- Anthropological and sociological studies have claimed time and again that we can only cope with being part of a tribe of 150 to 200 people. Anything more than that and we get confused and lose the intimacy of connection. Keep that in mind when aiming for too many followers!

7) Figure out who to follow. You will probably find you know quite a few people on Twitter. Using the menu tab on your page click on *'Who to Follow'*, and there are several ways to find people on Twitter, as follows:

- Use the *'Find Friends'* link to find people you know through your various Gmail, AOL, MSN, Hotmail and Yahoo! accounts.
- Use the *'View suggestions'* link for a wide range of possibilities that may, or may not, connect with your interests.

- Use the *'Browse Interests'* tab to find people by interest.

8) Look for people from organizations that you are in or for those that share a common interest. There are many business, companies, celebrities, and non-profit organizations on Twitter, ranging from Stephen Fry (@stephenfry) to Greenpeace (@greenpeace).

9) Create lists. If you're following lots of people, it can get hard to sift through all the *tweets*. For easy reference, you can organize the people you follow into a list. To add someone to a list, go to their profile. Then, click the person icon in the toolbar and select *"Add to List."* A menu with your lists will pop up; you can choose to create a new list or add the person to an existing one.

10) Upload a profile picture. This picture will be displayed with your name across the site. It must be a JPG, GIF, or PNG file and must be smaller than 700KB. To do so, click on *"settings"* in the drop down menu below your username. Then click on "Choose File" to select a file from your computer.

11) Add your name, location, and website. Under your profile picture, you have the choice to enter your full name. Adding a full name allows you to keep a professional aspect regardless of your username. You can also enter a location to let people know where you're tweeting from and link to your homepage or blog if you desire.

12) Work on your pithy 'Bio'. Make it eye-catching and interesting. Do it just right and it will help you build up followers; people thinking of following you do read the biographies to see if they have reason to follow you. Bear in mind that a biography can be up to 160 characters long, so you'll have to keep it short and to the point. Don't worry about typing your real name or website URL here--those can both be entered separately (as shown in the previous step).

13) Decide whether you want your tweets to be posted to Facebook. This can give you more view per tweet. If you so desire, click the *"Posts your Tweets to Facebook"* button at the bottom of the profile page.

[Author's Comments]

I personally wouldn't enable this feature. You may find yourself *tweeting* more often than you would posting to Facebook. If every *tweet* gets posted to Facebook it may look like you are spamming. I would however have my Facebook Posts automatically *tweet* on Twitter.

The same applies to having your tweets automatically upload to your Linkedin profile timeline. It can be very annoying when somebody seems to be bombarding you with tweets, from another social media platform.

14) Edit your language and time zone. Under the *"Account"* tab of settings, you have the ability to change the language and time zone that your Twitter is in. Do so by selecting the desired language and time zone from the drop down menus. You can also change your username and email address here if you ever need to.

15) Check the box below time zone to add a location to each of your Tweets. This is different than the location on your profile—it is specific to each *tweet* and can be as general as a town or as specific as your exact location. Even when this feature is enabled, you have the option to turn it on or off with each individual tweet.

16) Review the Tweet Media and Privacy settings. These are listed under the *Account* tab of your settings. Check the applicable boxes and hit save.

17) Change your password periodically. Protect your account by periodically changing your password. To do so, click on the *"Password"* tab under Settings. Enter your old password, then your new one twice. Hit *"Change"* when finished.

18) Decide when you want to receive emails from Twitter. Under the *"Notifications"* tab, there is a list of actions. Check the boxes next to those actions for which you'd like to receive an email.

19) Customize your profile. Every profile begins with the default background and color scheme. However, you can personalize it if you wish. Click on the *"Design"* tab of *Settings*. You can choose from one of the background images provided, or upload your own by clicking on the button that says *"Change Background Image."* Then, click on *"Choose File"* to upload one from your computer. You can also play with the color scheme by clicking *"Change Design Colors."*

20) Slide Into DMs. DMs are *direct messages*. They go straight to the intended person you are messaging. The DM feature uses an *inbox* and *outbox* system, but you are still limited to using 280 characters; you are also limited to sending *DMs* to only those users who follow you.

DMs cannot be seen by anyone other than yourself and the chosen recipient, and are thus more personal. To send a DM, go to the page of the follower you're sending one to, and click on the *"Message"* box.

- Be aware that some people really dislike *DMs* on Twitter because they reason that Twitter is an open conversation and a fast one, not a disguise for sending each other private messages. Also, *DMs* are not appreciated when they involve marketing or advertising.

[Author's Comments]

As a longtime Toastmaster and one who is working on honing my communication skills, I find the *DM* necessity of reducing a conversation to on 280 characters to be disturbing. Personal messages shouldn't be reduced this way. There is no room to add emotion or context to the message. I can see how brief messages intended to share some vital information is misunderstood by the receiver of the message.

21) Use third-party applications for ease of mobility and account sharing. Third-party applications such as TweetDeck and Twitter for iPhone (iPhone/iPod Touch/iPad), or UberSocial for Android formerly Twidroid (Android) can help you to manage your Twitter account(s) better. If you have lots of followers and if you follow lots of people, at which point it can be difficult to keep up with everything on Twitter's official website, you might want to try something a bit more advanced like Hoot Suite.

How to Use Twitter Effectively:

1) Understand what Twitter is and what it is not. Twitter is an on-line social networking place, like the watercooler of the Internet. It's a place of connection, friendships, and networking. Things that Twitter is <u>not</u> include assuming that it's nothing more than a sales forum (despite the many people who abuse this repeatedly), an obligatory add-on to your company's social media strategy without tending to it actively (daily!), or a place to spar with people.

- The mistake many people make is to dive right into Twitter and promote their website in nearly every single *tweet*. Big mistake! You wouldn't do that in real life, so don't do it on Twitter.
- The balance needs to be: more personal updates and less leads to things you want people to purchase.

Source: http://www.wikihow.com/Be-More-Popular-on-Twitter

2) Be authentic. Although the cliché "be yourself" is a bit overdone, it's highly applicable to Twitter.

Followers trust you are presenting yourself genuinely and this will only resonate where you give of yourself to other people. As in real life, it's important to be interesting, and to be interested in others.

- Provide your real name and occupation or interests. This builds up a bigger picture of who you really are and reassures your followers. Don't say anything that would bore your follows. You need them to be "happy"
- If possible, provide a link in your Twitter profile to work you're doing on-line or to something that tells more about you on-line (such as Linkedin or Facebook).
- Customize your Twitter photo and background. Twitter followers don't like seeing the standard Twitter bird as a photo - use one of yourself or something that identifies clearly with you. In addition, add your own colors and maybe even designs or photos to enliven the background of your Twitter page.

Source: http://www.wikihow.com/Be-More-Popular-on-Twitter

3) Interact. Twitter is about relationships and friendships. You can grow to know a lot of amazing people through your Twitter account just by interacting with them regularly, and many will become firm friends even though you've never actually met them.

- Be sure to reply to all @ messages. If your name is mentioned, it means someone cares enough to include you, and it's important to acknowledge this by replying.
- Retweet (RT) people's information regularly and with consistency. This is the lifeblood of Twitter, the sharing of information through retweeting. It's a form of respect and a way of acknowledging that the person being retweeted is sharing information worthy of retweeting about.
- Communicate with Twitter users who are already popular. If they notice you and like what they see, they'll help you in your 'social media climbing' by sharing your information with their followers, and hopefully recommending you as well.
- Leave your Twitter address with comments that you make on blog sites so that people can work their way back to the real you and learn more.

Source: http://www.wikihow.com/Be-More-Popular-on-Twitter

4) Provide information other people want to know and share. You'll only be retweeted and followed if you're providing a Twitter stream that grabs people's attention.

Once you've established yourself as someone who shares certain types of information, be sure to keep providing fresh, fascinating, and curious updates.

- Include links to interesting stories, news items, websites, recipes, etc.
- Also send links to photos, videos, and other visual treats for followers to look at. Cute animals are often a winner as light relief!

- Keep the updates flowing at a regular pace so that people know they can turn to you reliably.
- If a disaster or major event happens in your locality or country, don't be afraid to switching to it in addition to, or in place of your normal *tweets*. Share updates and useful information such as phone numbers, emergency information, and shelter addresses, etc. People will readily share this information with your name on it, and you can easily end up meeting many people who are in the thick of providing emergency services, grateful for your support in getting the information out.
- Bake some Twitter cookies and share the recipe link and the photos of your resulting cookies with your followers.

Source: http://www.wikihow.com/Be-More-Popular-on-Twitter

5) Build your popularity. To be popular, you will need more and more followers, people who are retweeting your information, and singing your praises to their followers.

- Follow people. Do this as a daily ritual by focusing on people you have things in common with. Use the Twitter search engine to find people with similar interests; key in words that are likely to make appropriate returns such as 'Super Bowl', 'vegan', 'burlesque', 'cheese', 'mom', etc.
- Half the fun is in finding new people "just like you"!
- Follow back those who follow you. Regularly add new people to those you follow, as well as regularly adding people who have added you.
- Use automated follower adder tools if wished. If you decide to pay for more followers, be sure that there is a benefit in doing so, for your business, brand, or image, etc. For most individuals, payment is unnecessary; use your time and personal effort wisely instead.
- Monitor your popularity using tools that tell you your popularity status. There are many tools available for this, and they can be focused on country, region, topic (such as "Top LA

Tweeters", "Top Green Tweeters", etc.), or other elements you're keen to know about.

6) Reward your followers. There are a number of ways to reward your Twitter followers that will impress them and have them tooting your horn with their followers. Some of the ways include:

- Use the #FollowFriday (#FF) mechanism to list the names of your favorite followers by way of thanks, and as a way of getting their names circulated. In turn, your name gets circulated when they thank you or reuse your #FF list directly.
- Tailor individual thanks to your followers. Personalizing thanks is impressive; it not only thrills the person you're thanking but it makes other followers think you're someone who cares about people individually and this is an important impression to make. One great way of doing this is to pick up portions of their profile and to say thanks by replicating this person's main points. For example, "My gratitude to @BilbowikiHow - a social media guru with a heart of gold who specializes in horticulture, laughter yoga, & Dr Who memorabilia. Please follow"
- Say thanks to your followers in a blog. Make it really special by singling out particular followers for your blog post. Write a small piece on who they are, what they do, and why they rock. Include their photo and a link back to Twitter. And then let them and your other followers know via Twitter! This one is always loved and shows you really do care about them. The added benefit is that your blog also gets greater coverage as followers share it on.

Source: http://www.wikihow.com/Be-More-Popular-on-Twitter

7) Always focus on the purpose of Twitter as being about connectedness. Any time you feel like promoting yourself endlessly, pull back and remember that Twitter is about connecting and relating, not about selling teeth whitener to your pals. The networks of friendship created on-line are as real as offline friendships for many people.

Just as it is easy to wear out friendships by asking friends one time too many to support your Tupperware or Avon sales, so too this wearies friends on-line. Keep the selling to a minimum, and ratchet up the connecting, sharing, and Twitter loving.

Source: http://www.wikihow.com/Be-More-Popular-on-Twitter

8) Tweet things that people can relate to. No one wants to hear about your complaints all the time, so try to tweet some positive things. Also, following your followers shows people that if they follow you, then they also gain a follower.

Source: http://www.wikihow.com/Be-More-Popular-on-Twitter

FINAL THOUGHTS ON TWITTER:

I have been using Twitter for several years now to promote my Toastmasters club on-line. While I think that is a great on-line social media tool for providing reach for the messages I have to share with the world, or at least my local community, I believe it has fallen short of driving visitors to our club. I have yet to hear from anyone "Oh, we saw you on Twitter and we just had to come and check you out!"

While having a large number of people following you would seem to indicate social proof in some people's mind, I believe as in Facebook and Linkedin, there is a race going on to see who can amass the most followers. Your *tweets* would tend to get lost in most of your *Follower's* timelines unless they had a specific interest in what you were tweeting and actively followed you. I would rather have a smaller number of engaged, interactive *Followers*, than a large number of unengaged ones.

Your Twitter *branding* needs to be consistent and interconnected with your club's website and any other marketing initiatives you have going. It has to be easy to access and serve a purpose of encouraging potential guests to your club to take further action.

Social media is time consuming. Twitter just as much as any of the others. I believe the way to make it easier for you to use for our purposes of attracting members to our clubs as well as special events that we may be hosting is to systematize the process. I've advised against having your *tweets* automatically post to your Facebook, however Facebook to Twitter works great. As I described earlier in the section on Facebook, there are some excellent sources of information that you can share by *tweeting*, to attract attention to your cause. As I write this paragraph I'm thinking it is a lot like fishing. You dangle some desirable bait in front of a fish hoping they will bite. The content we post to our social media venues is the bait. We can only hope that our *Followers* bite and let us land them as club members.

I don't like seeing important conversations that should be taking place in person, or at least in an explanatory e-mail, being reduced to 280 characters and relying on the off chance that I check my Twitter account to receive the message. To me, that flies in the face of the communication skills we are trying to develop in Toastmasters.

On-line social media interaction started off to further conversations between like-minded individuals. It has evolved into marketing mayhem. I guess I can leave the question with you, "If everybody else is doing it... should you be tweeting too?"

IN THE NEXT CHAPTER WE LOOK AT USING INSTAGRAM FOR ON-LINE self-promotion.

INSTAGRAM
INSTAGRAM

From Wikipedia, the free encyclopedia:

INSTAGRAM IS AN ON-LINE PHOTO AND VIDEO SHARING SOCIAL networking service. It allows users to take pictures and videos, apply digital filters to them, and share them to their followers. They can then share them on a variety of social networking services, such as Facebook, Twitter, Tumblr and Flickr. A feature is that it confines photos to a square shape, similar to Kodak Instamatic and Polaroid images. This is different from the 16:9 aspect ratio typically used by digital cameras. Users are also able to record and share short videos lasting for up to 15 seconds.

The PEW Survey [Pew Research Center Internet & Technology 2018] indicated over 33% of US adults use Instagram.

Advantages:

- Provides an instant snapshot of an idea or concept for those that are visually minded.
- Usually visually appealing, attracts your attention quickly.
- Easily allows branding to be incorporated.
- Easily shared.
- If a picture says a thousand words... an Instagram with words & graphics can say considerably more.

Disadvantages/Considerations:

- Requires significant graphic artistry skills to create a professional-looking graphic.
- Requires logistical & strategic thinking skills to convey the message you want.
- Inappropriate choice of colors in your graphic may elicit the wrong emotional response in your viewer than you intended.
- Not everybody likes 'big picture' graphics.
- Many Instagrams don't seem to have an actual purpose or leave you wondering if the message might have been better created/crafted differently.
- Creating content can be time consuming.

Instagram is optimized for mobile devices. Like other social media platforms, you follow people and hopefully they will follow you in return.

Smartphone apps allow you to take photos and videos up to 15 seconds in length. The app does the timing for you. You just aim and press the record button. Once your photo or video is taken, you are given the option of which social media platform you want to post to.

I'll admit to being a newby with this social media platform. I had in my mind it was strictly for sharing or promoting graphics that you or somebody else had created. I now see the ability it has to share photos.

I can see the advantages of capturing photos of your business activities in action, hopefully with everyone having a good time, and being able to immediately post to your favorite social media platform.

Once again, your message would be posted to your *Instagram Timeline* as well and anybody that follows you would have it appear in their feed.

I can also see the advantage of posting business-related content to your Instagram account in that people that follow you will be exposed to your brand and/or your business.

How to Self-promote/market Yourself on Instagram.

Post Quality Content:

Your photos, comments, videos and other information posted on Instagram must be of high quality. If it's not, no one will give it a second glance.

Regardless of the shape of your photo, Instagram posts it as a square. You might need to do some cropping of your photo before uploading to avoid important elements being left out by Instagram.

Instagram requires your photos to be of certain pixels if you want to have quality images. Square images, for instance, must be 1080 x 1080 pixels.

Finally, the photos themselves must have relevance. They should be unique, beautiful and interesting.

Create Engaging Content:

On top of being exquisite, posted media should also be engaging. Know your target audience and appeal to their likes and dislikes.

To do this, post information your audience wants to hear. Give touching client feedback, photos of customers using your product or images of readers following your blog advice.

Ask questions to spark conversations and reply to individuals who reach out.

Don't forget about videos. Over half of the population watch on-line videos every day. Posting a quick tutorial or a story is an easy way to promote your blog.

Use Hashtags:

Hashtags aren't going away anytime soon.

Hashtags make your posts discoverable and easy to find or share. They are a great way to promote your blog.

The key with hashtags is to use them wisely; don't tack on 15 hashtags to your image because you hope it will make it appear more frequently. It won't.

Instead, research which hashtags are trending and which are being used by competitors. Then include a couple hashtags with your post.

Try to use hashtags that promote action, such as readers taking photos of themselves or doing something for a contest. This drives views.

Promote With Other Social Media:

Chances are you have a Facebook, Linkedin or YouTube account. The truth is, most people are just like you. In fact, recent surveys indicate the average person has seven social media accounts.

Therefore, it's only logical to cross-use your platforms. Include links to your Instagram account on your blog or Facebook. Likewise, lead Instagram users to helpful articles or fun activities through other platforms.

Forge Relationships:

Don't ever take advantage of Instagram and view it as only a means to achieve a wider audience base. As soon as you do, readers will smell it a mile away.

Instead, approach Instagram as a fun outlet through which you can engage with new individuals. To do that, form a relationship with users.

Ask questions and respond to comments. Post fun photos or videos from your followers on your site with a short link to the user's original post.

In doing this, you create a sincere relationship with your audience. People respond to this.

Humanize Your Brand:

Make your Instagram posts more personal. Don't be shy about showing what goes on behind the scenes.

Multiple studies find that individuals are less trusting of businesses or people seeking only to promote something. Don't fall into these groups. Instead, share about yourself and your blog so that Instagram users see you are a person, not a robotic corporation lacking empathy.

To do this, consider posting behind-the-scenes photos depicting what a certain article entailed or an action you took connected to the blog.

Get friends in on it, too. Show who you are so that your personality shines through your brand.

Take Advantage of Insights:

Insights is a service offered for individuals who create or transfer personal accounts to business profiles on Instagram. It compiles demographics about your followers, viewers, and more into an easy-to-read format.

For bloggers wanting to promote their site, this is invaluable.

By using Insights, you get a closer view of your audience. This makes it easier to find hashtags, create interesting and eye-catching topics and even analyze what works and doesn't work.

Buddy Up:

Our last piece of advice is also one that always increases growth: buddy up.

By that, we mean reach out to your friends and colleagues who use Instagram and other social media platforms. Ask them if they would be interested in linking to your site when appropriate and do the same for them.

In this way, both you and your acquaintances obtain free publicity.

Another great way to reach new viewers is through an influencer. An influencer is anyone who has a large following on social media, in this case Instagram.

Contact individuals and ask them to read your best articles or, if you're a business, offer them a free product. Then, request that they give your article or product an honest review–so make whatever is provided amazing and noteworthy.

Many influencers use an Instagram growth service; that means they get professional input on what hashtags to use, when to post and what to post. It also means they have many loyal followers and are up-to-date on the latest trends, so buddying with one is an invaluable way to reach thousands of individuals.

Source: https://www.onblastblog.com/get-instafamous-how-to-market-yourself-on-instagram/

IN OUR NEXT CHAPTER WE LOOK AT PINTEREST.

PINTEREST

Pinterest is a web and mobile application company, which operates an eponymous photo sharing website. Registration is required for use. The site was founded by Ben Silbermann, Paul Sciarra and Evan Sharp. It is managed by Cold Brew Labs and funded by a small group of entrepreneurs and investors.

Pinterest CEO Ben Silbermann summarized the company as a "catalog of ideas" rather than as a social network that inspires users to "go out and do that thing."

Source: Wikipedia, the free encyclopedia

"Pinterest is a highly visual virtual pinboard site that lets you "pin" or collect images from the Web. You create boards to help you categorize your images and add descriptions to remind you why you bookmarked them in the first place."

Source: PC Mag http://www.pcmag.com/article2/0,2817,2418047,00.asp

Author's Comments:

Eponoymous? For all the Grammarians out there, according to Merriam –Webster On-line Dictionary... "of, relating to, or being the person or thing for whom or which something is named: of relating to, or being an eponym."

Which of course begs the question "what is the definition of eponym?"

Once again from Merriam –Webster On-line Dictionary "one for whom or which something is or is believed to be named"

It seems like a convoluted way to say they are a photo sharing website.

While the owners of Pinterest say they are not a social media site, they still encourage their members sharing i.e. pinning, building a following and following others in turn.

In order to research this chapter, I opened my own Pinterest account to see if there was value in doing so.

The basics of Pinterest are as follows:

You join Pinterest: Joining is easy. It will ask you to join by connecting with Facebook or Twitter. If you have either of these accounts in place, you can do so. If you don't, you can still join using your e-mail address.

To connect with Facebook, you will need to give the app permission to access your basic info, email address, birthday, and likes. This lets the app post activity on your behalf, though you can decide whether your pins get reposted to Facebook. It automatically imports your Facebook photo; you can then create a username and password. Here you can uncheck or leave checked two boxes: "Follow recommended friends" and "Publish activity to Facebook Timeline."

By connecting with Twitter, you're giving the app permission to read tweets from your timeline, see who you follow and follow new people, update your profile, and post tweets for you.

If you sign up with your email, instead, you'll be asked a few more questions such as your gender since that info isn't imported from an existing social media account. Upload a profile photo and proceed.

Follow Some Boards: Once you have an account, you'll need to find fascinating boards to fill your feed. Pinterest gets you started by suggesting some. Select a category from the list such as Design, Geek, Science & Nature, and Technology among others, and then check at least five boards to continue. You don't have to keep the ones they suggest for you.

Keep in mind most accounts have multiple boards, so if you follow an account you automatically follow all its boards. You can also follow specific boards, and can unfollow a board at any time without the account being notified.

Verify Your Account: After selecting some boards, you'll receive an email confirmation.

Once you verify your account, the next screen you'll see is your *home feed*, which features the most recent pins from people you follow. The more users or boards you follow, the more content will turn over.

Adjust Account Settings: The next thing to do is to adjust your settings. Mouse over the drop-down menu in the upper right-hand corner with your picture and click *Settings*. Here you can update basic information, opt out of email notifications, and connect or disconnect your Facebook or Twitter account.

Create Your Own Boards: You need to build boards in order to collect and organize items you're interested in. To do so, click *Your Boards* in the upper right-hand drop-down menu, then click *Create a Board*. A box will pop up asking you to name your board, add a description, and categorize it.

For an in-depth, easy to follow explanation of how to use Pinterest I would suggest visiting WikiHow to do anything http://www.wikihow.com/Use-Pinterest

For my own account, I set up the following Boards:

- Leadership
- Storytelling
- Presentation Skills

- Toastmasters World Champion of Public Speaking
- Toastmasters Marketing Ideas
- Business Networking
- Rae Stonehouse
- Team Work
- Entrepreneurs
- Pin Now, Read Later

Following other Pinterest boards can be a good source of content. Another useful tool is to add a Pinterest pin button to your browser. This allows you to pin any graphic you encounter on your web travels and post it to one of the boards you have created in your account.

Another option is to create a business account for your business or personal brand. One of the first steps is to add it to a category of business.

Once you create your account, it will include a contact e-mail and the name of your 'business', you will be prompted to create some boards.

In an on-line search for Pinterest, I found individual member's boards being listed. At this point, I don't know how the search engines determine whose boards to list. Perhaps it is by number of followers?

Final Words on Pinterest:

While the Pinterest developers say they aren't a social media site, they do rely on social sharing for their success. Having a Pinterest account for your business or personal brand is an additional 'touchpoint' for someone to discover you.

Whether your community has a large Pinterest following, if any, remains to be seen. Businesses are finding creative ways to use Pinterest to share their messages every day. Perhaps in time it will be of use to us.

As I said earlier, I haven't used Pinterest enough to determine the value for my own self-promotion. As an author, I'm led to believe there can be an advantage to me promoting my books and e-courses on Pinterest.

In the next chapter we look at YouTube.

YOUTUBE

We've talked about the advantages of using Facebook to link to videos that are already uploaded to YouTube, both yours and others. In this chapter we look at how you can use video for self-promotion and marketing.

As in other chapters, I'm going to use my Toastmasters club as an example of the points I want to cover.

You don't need to register to watch YouTube videos, however you do if you want to upload them. All registered YouTube users can upload videos up to 15 minutes in duration.

Users who have a good record of complying with the site's Community Guidelines may be offered the ability to upload videos up to 12 hours in length, which requires verifying the account, normally through a mobile phone. I didn't find this to be an onerous task.

YouTube allows you to upload video that has been recorded in multiple formats.

YouTube's slogan from 2005 to 2012 was "Broadcast Yourself." That slogan is really the essence of why it is worth our while to create a YouTube channel to promote your Toastmaster's club. We want to broadcast to the world, or at least our community, that our Toastmasters club is worthwhile visiting and joining.

Advantages:

- Huge global brand recognition.
- Relatively easy to upload videos.
- Easy to share videos created and/or uploaded by others.
- Viewable on multiple devices.
- Relatively easy to create your own channel.
- Has the ability to brand your videos.
- Gives your video an implied credibility "If it's on YouTube, it must be good!"
- Allows you to develop a following, i.e. fans.
- Helps you to stand out from other businesses.
- Advancements in electronics e.g., smart phones, allow almost everyone to become a videographer

Disadvantages/Considerations:

- Longer videos can take a long time to upload, sometimes up to a day.
- It's easy to get your content 'lost in the crowd.'
- It takes time to promote your channel.
- Effective, semi-professional quality video requires an understanding of sound & lighting principles.
- While it may be easy to shoot video, effective editing requires skills and time.
- Takes time and effort to share your content on-line.

While it can be easy to create your own YouTube Channel and start uploading videos, deciding if it is an effective use of your time and effort to raise awareness of your Toastmasters club, is another story. Like all the other social media venues we have explored, the answer is "it depends."

On-line videos seem to be easily indexed by search engines. We will explore in a while how to optimize your videos so they will be indexed by the search engines and how to ensure they will be featured when someone searches for your Toastmasters club. But before we get there, let's take a look at videoing in greater detail.

Utilizing Video in your Toastmasters Club:

A typical Toastmasters club meeting provides lots of opportunities to utilize video. As a learning tool, speakers who are delivering a presentation from the Toastmasters Communication Program, could be videoed, for later evaluation and constructive feedback.

Your newer members may not be comfortable viewing the video, however video can be an effective tool for an experienced speaker wanting to fast track their speaking skill development.

We are getting used to watching video, yet some people may feel uncomfortable with the video when they are the featured subject. One of the problems new speakers often experience with viewing video of their presentations is they tend to focus on what they view to be their deficiencies, short comings or mistakes. An experienced Toastmaster evaluator or professional speech coach would instead focus on the strengths of the speaker they observe and encourage the speaker to strengthen the skills they have.

Speech evaluators could also be videoed for future analysis. Those videos could form the basis of an educational session on how to effectively evaluate speeches.

As we discussed in the section about Facebook, it is possible to upload your video directly to Facebook without having to upload to YouTube first. The rule of thumb or what seems to be effective is to create shorter videos and upload them directly to Facebook. These videos should be crafted so they encourage the viewer to check out the longer version of the video which is posted to YouTube.

As many people are using mobile devices and smart phones to access their social media, the shorter length video can be an effective way to attract more attention to you or your Toastmasters club.

Creating good quality video has become well within the reach of many of our Toastmaster's club members. For example, an inexpensive tripod stand and bracket can be purchased that supports a smart phone on a desktop. Many of our members have camcorders as they have become quite affordable in recent years.

Creating good quality video also entails ensuring you have adequate lighting on your subject as well as being able to capture the sound effectively. A past room my Toastmaster's club met in was very challenging in that the overhead lighting was poor for video recording purposes. It left the speaker in the dark.

As well, my camcorder records all the background noise with the video. Most of the time we are not aware of background noises such as air conditioners/heating systems or noises from elsewhere in the building. The camcorder hears it though, and it can become quite evident when you review the video.

One solution to the sound problem, although not necessarily an inexpensive one, is to have your speaker use a wireless lapel mic called a lavalier mic. I understand many professional video producers are moving away from these mics in the belief they create a hollow sound. They recommend using an additional, out of sight, sound recording device, capturing the audio from the presenter. This can be easily done.

I've done it a few times by using a smart phone to capture the audio, then replacing the sound track in post-production that the video camera created.

In addition to the lighting challenge I described above, I have found difficulties with recording a presenter who was working with a Power-Point presentation to display slides to illustrate or add to their presentation. Moving the camera back and forth from the speaker to the screen, while shooting the video, was quite distracting. The differences in the lighting on the speaker and in the projection screen caused problems with the recording, as there was often a brief period of lens adjustment.

I solved this problem by keeping the camera focused on the speaker only, rather than going back and forth, adding the PowerPoint slides during the post-production phase.

Post Production: While going in to any depth on how to process your video is beyond the scope of this book, it is well within the reach of anyone with the time and inclination to do so.

Consumer-grade video editing software has come down in price, and there are some good products out there. I have had good success with Sony Movie Studio. I also use Techsmith's Camtasia for many of my educational videos.

You can even get an app that allows you to edit your video directly on your smart phone, without having to download to your computer and also to upload to the Internet or to send it to someone.

There is one school of thought that says there is value in uploading your raw, unedited videos as it makes you seem more natural. On the other hand, the post production editing allows you to build in transitions, title slides and branding.

A technique for creating good quality titles I have had success with is to create them in PowerPoint, then import them and install them in your video. I'm sure there are other ways to do so, perhaps within the video editing software itself. Fadeins and fadeouts can be added to make your video professional looking.

Creating a YouTube Channel for Your Toastmaster's Club:

Creating a YouTube Channel for your Toastmaster's club is easily done. The instructions for doing so are readily available on line, so I'm not going to go into great detail in showing you how to do it, other than commenting on some features you should be aware of.

Uploading videos of your fellow Toastmasters in action can serve as a good promotional tool for visitors to your YouTube Channel. It can help a guest get to know club members even before they actually meet them for the first time.

Other ideas to draw attention to your channel are to create "themed" playlists. For my club's channel I have created Playlists for *"Toastmasters World Champions of Public Speaking Winning Speeches"* where I feature videos that I have found on-line of contest-winning speeches. Watching and emulating speaking champions can be a great way to develop your presentation skills. As I mentioned earlier, these videos can serve as an educational tool for your Toastmasters meeting when added to a facilitated educational session.

Another playlist is entitled *"Presentation Skills Development."* As I have the time, I review and add videos to this list that I believe offer good advice or instructional value. These videos of speeches are good to schedule as uploads to your Facebook Page to keep your followers interested in your Facebook page and hopefully come out to visit your club.

A notable link on the YouTube navigational bar is the *About* link.

When you set up your channel, you are able to add details to help with its promotion.

As posted in YouTube Help on-line:

A YouTube channel provides a single place to organize your video content for your audience. As a channel owner, you can add videos, playlists, and information about yourself or your channel for visitors to explore. Your channel will be broken into the following areas:

- **Home** is where your audience arrives when they see your channel for the first time. Here, your audience can view a feed of your activities or preview different sections containing your content if you have enabled the browse view.
- **Videos** shows a list of all your public uploads and all of the videos you have publicly liked. You can filter by most popular or date added.
- **Playlists** contains a list of all the playlists that you have created.
- **Discussion**, if enabled in your channel navigation settings, will display comments left on your channel.

- **About** lets you add a channel description (maximum length of 1000 characters), set your channel country, enter a business contact email address, and define social or other web links.

Links you add here are featured just below your description and use the icon from the corresponding social network when displayed. You can overlay up to five of these links on your channel art as shortcut icons, or favicons.

Additional custom links may be entered but will only appear below your description. You are able to customize the name of the link (how it appears on your channel) when entering your links.

To edit any of these items on your *About* tab, hover over the content, then click the edit icon.

As in other social media platforms, you need to promote your channel and provide links so viewers can easily find you. Cross-promote on all of your social media and web properties.

Optimizing Your Videos for Search Engines:

YouTube SEO Tips

- Rename your video file using a target keyword.
- Insert your keyword naturally in the video title.
- Optimize your video description.
- Tag your video with popular keywords that relate to your topic.
- Categorize your video.
- Upload a custom thumbnail image for your video's result link.

For more details, visit https://blog.hubspot.com/marketing/youtube-seo

Final Thoughts on YouTube:

YouTube is growing every day. There is a phenomenal amount of videos being uploaded every minute from around the world.

BLOW YOUR OWN HORN!

It has been called the fourth biggest search engine, and other search engines are doing a good job of indexing videos. If you have a promotional video for your club or your business uploading it to YouTube could be beneficial if you publicize the link to it.

With so many videos on YouTube, it's easy to have your video get lost. Be sure to cross-promote it and have appropriate tags added to your videos so they do come up when somebody is searching for Toastmasters, public speaking, communication skill development and leadership.

I recently discovered a perfect example of how cross-promotion works. I had uploaded a video of a Toastmaster's club officer training session I had conducted on the subject of conflict management related to Toastmasters to our club YouTube channel. I was doing an Internet search for my club and was surprised to find my video posted on a site for Rotary International. This, in essence, gave a plug for Toastmasters in a completely different organization.

In the next chapter we look at blogging for self-promotion.

BLOGS VS NEWSLETTERS

From Wikipedia: A blog (a truncation of the expression weblog) is a discussion or informational site published on the World Wide Web and consisting of discrete entries ('posts') typically displayed in reverse chronological order (the most recent post appears first).

A majority are interactive, allowing visitors to leave comments and even message each other via GUI widgets on the blogs, and it is this interactivity that distinguishes them from other static websites. In that sense, blogging can be seen as a form of social networking service.

Many blogs provide commentary on a particular subject; others function as more personal on-line diaries; others function more as on-line brand advertising of a particular individual or company. A typical blog combines text, images, and links to other blogs, Web pages, and other media related to its topic.

The ability of readers to leave comments in an interactive format is an important contribution to the popularity of many blogs. Most blogs are primarily textual, although some focus on art (art blogs), photographs (photoblogs), videos (video blogs or 'vlogs'), music (MP3 blogs), and audio (podcasts). Microblogging is another type of blogging, featuring very short posts. In education, blogs can be used as instructional resources. These blogs are referred to as edublogs.

Blogs have been around since the 1990s and have evolved to the point that almost anyone can create and publish one.

It would certainly help if you have good writing skills to produce a blog that shows your you, your personal brand and/or your business in a good light, however you can work around a lack of skills by creating the material and having someone with better skills edit and polish it for you.

As for content for your blog, the topics are endless. You likely have a wealth of experience you can draw from.

Some will argue that an effective blog should be in the 250 to 500 word range, short and sweet. I'm not one of them. My personal belief is that to explore a subject and describe it in the manner it deserves requires a few more words. Most of my blogs are in the 1800 to 2500 word range.

I've included some of my How's Your Net Working Blog posts in the Resource Section.

Writing your article can be the easy part, at least it has been for me. Posting it and promoting the article can be the more challenging part.

At its basis, your blog article needs to be hosted somewhere on the Internet. If you have your own website in place and you have the skills to upload content yourself or access to someone who does, you can post your content there.

The next step is to promote your blog post. It's fine and dandy, as they say, that you have created a masterpiece, but if nobody reads it, then what good is it? Here is where social media comes in.

If you have a personal or business profile on Linkedin, you can upload the title, promotional copy and the url to your article to the timeline. You can also post a notification of your blog to Groups that you are a member and that the blog would be appropriate for and hopefully well received.

You can do the same for your personal or business Facebook Page. It can be a good place to post your blogs if you don't have access to anywhere else. As I have described earlier in the Facebook chapter, your blogs are a good example of content that you can post to local Facebook Pages and Groups, if you belong to them.

Twitter provides you with the same promotional opportunities. Either add it to the Twitterfeed and post or if you have set up your Facebook Page to automatically tweet your Facebook Posts on Twitter, let it do so.

There are other on-line places that you can post your blog either free or at a fee. Other blogging services worthwhile checking out are: WordPress, Tumblr and Blogger.

From Wikipedia:

WordPress.com is a blog web hosting service provider owned by Automattic, and powered by the open source WordPress software.] It provides free blog hosting for registered users and is financially supported via paid upgrades, "VIP" services and advertising.

Tumblr is a microblogging platform and social networking website founded by David Karp and owned by Yahoo! Inc. The service allows users to post multimedia and other content to a short-form blog. Users can follow other users' blogs, as well as make their blogs private. Much of the website's features are accessed from the 'dashboard' interface, where the option to post content and posts of followed blogs appear.

Blogger is a blog-publishing service that allows multi-user blogs with time-stamped entries. It was developed by Pyra Labs, which was bought by Google in 2003. Generally, the blogs are hosted by Google at a subdomain of blogspot.com. Blogs can also be hosted in the registered custom domain of the blogger (like www.example.com). So blogspot.com domain publishings will be redirected to the custom domain. A user can have up to 100 blogs per account.

Wherever you decide to host your blog an important element to its success is the ability for readers to comment on the content. Social media platforms allow readers to post comments on content posted to their timelines. The challenge for you is to monitor the places you have posted your blog and respond to the commenter in a timely manner. Your comments hopefully will engage the reader, both the ones who have commented and subsequent ones that are read by later readers, to take further action. Following up with appropriate and timely comments can help increase your credibility on the subject you have written about.

And then there's newsletters.

From Mr. Google... A blog stays on your website and can be seen by anyone. You send out your email newsletter by email to a specific group of people. Blogs help you position yourself and your company as an industry expert. Email Newsletters allow you to track and target specific group of readers.

Both email newsletters and blogs allow you to communicate effectively with prospects, leads, and customers in different ways.

Here's the differences between a blog and a newsletter.

Source: https://www.xzito.com/blog/blog-vs-email-newsletter-which-strategy-works-best

Blog

A blog stays on your website and can be seen by anyone.

Email Newsletter

You send out your email newsletter by email to a specific group of people.

∾

BLOG

Blogs help you position yourself and your company as an industry expert.

Email Newsletter

Email Newsletters allow you to track and target specific group of readers.

~

Blog

Blogs are often used to educate your prospective customers about your product/service, and move them through the sales funnel.

Email Newsletter

Email newsletters help nurture existing leads and customers, and keep your business top-of-mind.

~

Blog

Blogs are forever. They remain live on the web until you take them down or stop paying for hosting.

Email Newsletter

They are gone once they are sent.

~

Blog

Each blog post is considered to be a new web page, increasing your reach, popularity, and ranking within the search engines.

Email Newsletter

Email newsletters are not new web pages.

~

Blog

Your blogs can be shared on social media networks. This sharing allows you to build links and be more relevant and visible to search engines; helping you increase your ranking on the search results.

Email Newsletter

Email newsletters can be forwarded. However, search engines don't acknowledge email forwards as much as they do with social media sharing.

FROM A SELF-PROMOTIONAL PERSPECTIVE, THERE ARE ADVANTAGES TO creating both blogs and newsletters.

With newsletters, you own the list. If you are marketing a product or a service, it is often said "the money is in your list!"

A concept called 'permission-based marketing' is in effect when someone signs up for your newsletter. They are in essence giving you permission to market to them in return for something you have promised them.

Your newsletter can be a good way to communicate with your followers and anybody who has shown an interest in you and a desire to know more. If you are an author, your newsletter could update your fans about upcoming book releases or perhaps what was behind the scenes as inspiration for previous books you have written and published.

IN THE NEXT CHAPTER WE LOOK AT QUORA.COM AS A SELF-promotion tool.

QUORA.COM

You may not have heard of Quora.com. I usually have to give a quick explanation of what they are when I talk to someone about it and why there is value.

Basically, it is an on-line site that allows members to post questions and for self-proclaimed experts to answer the questions with facts or opinions.

It can be a good source of answers for questions you have or an excellent way to promote yourself as a content expert on a global basis.

Here is a brief overview of Quora.com. I'll provide my thoughts on Quora at the end of this chapter.

According to Wikipedia - The Free Encyclopedia, Quora is an American question-and-answer website where questions are asked, answered, and edited by Internet users, either factually or in the form of opinions.

Users can collaborate by editing questions and suggesting edits to answers that have been submitted by other users.

In September 2018, Quora reported that it was receiving 300 million unique visitors every month.

Quora requires users to register with the complete form of their real names rather than an Internet pseudonym (screen name); although verification of names is not required, false names can be reported by the community. This was done with the ostensible intent of adding credibility to answers. Users with a certain amount of activity on the website have the option to write their answers anonymously, but not by default.

Currently, Quora has different ways to recommend questions to users:

Home feed question recommendations

In this method, users have a *timeline* that is personalized to their preferences. Quora also provides 'interesting' questions that are relevant to those preferences.

Daily digest

In this method, Quora sends a daily email containing a set of questions with one answer that is deemed the best answer, given certain ranking criteria.

Related questions

In this method, a set of questions that relates to the current question is displayed on the side. This display is not tailored to the specific user.

Requested answers

This feature lets a user direct a question to other users whom they consider better suited to answer it.

Content moderation

Quora supports various features to moderate content posted by users. The majority of content moderation is done by the users, though staff can also intervene.

Upvote and downvote

Users can rank answers based on how relevant or helpful they found the answers to be. This feature is intended to help maintain the quality of content posted on-line. The more upvotes an answer receives, the higher it is ranked, and it shows up on top of the searches related to the question. If an answer is ranked poorly, it is 'collapsed' and will not show up in people's feeds.

Report answer

Users can report plagiarism, harassment, spam, and factually incorrect articles, etc. This is intended to keep sub-standard content under check.

Suggest edits

Users propose changes to an answer. The proposed changes are made visible to the author of the answer who can either approve (and publish) or reject them.

Edit question and source

Users can directly edit a question. These changes are reviewed by Quora Moderation, which can revert them if they are deemed unconstructive.

Top Writers Program

In November 2012, Quora introduced the Top Writers Program as a way to recognize individuals who had made especially valuable content contributions to the site and encourage them to continue. About 150 writers were chosen each year. Top writers were invited to occasional exclusive events and received gifts such as branded clothing items and books. The company believed that by cultivating a group of core users who were particularly invested in the site, a positive feedback loop of user engagement would be created.

Partner program

In 2018, Quora introduced a program that offers incentives to users that ask questions. Members of the program, who are chosen by invitation only, are paid via Stripe or PayPal, based on user engagement and advertising revenue generated by the questions.

"Questions are compensated based on the user engagement and advertising revenue they generate. After you ask a question, you will earn money on it for 1 year."

This program has been roundly criticized by member users who feel that the financial incentive has led to the posting of questions of an inferior quality that have corrupted the original concept of the site.

Spaces

In November 2018, Quora ended support of user blogs and introduced a new feature called 'Spaces'. Spaces are communities of like-minded people where users can discuss and share content related to the space topic or subject. A space is a Quora page which has its own administrators, moderators, contributors, and followers.

Administrators have absolute control of the space. Moderators can add or delete and approve or decline content and submissions to the space. Contributors can add content such as posts, external website links, or Quora questions and answers.

Once a space has acquired a certain number of followers (2000 as of August 2019), Quora allows the space's administrator to add a custom URL, beginning with "q/".

Final Thoughts on Quora

I joined Quora in August 2016 and have answered some 900 questions since then. As I write this section, I have reached one million answer views.

Early in 2019 I was awarded a Top Writer in 2018 distinction. As well as bragging rights, I received a year subscription to the on-line version of the New York Times. I passed the subscription on to my son as he had more interest in it than I did.

You can choose which areas of questioning you want to participate in. I actively answer questions in the following categories:

Public Speaking; Toastmasters International; Career Advice; Interpersonal Interaction; Speeches; Human Behaviour; Self-Improvement; Personal Networking; Understanding Human Behaviour; Job Searches; Linkedin Profiles; Business Relationships; Business Networking; Shyness; Business Cards; Entrepreneurship; Meetings; Medicine and Healthcare, Nurses, Master of Ceremonies.

Whew! I hadn't realized I was an expert in so many areas. [... said tongue in cheek].

Quora provides a good opportunity for you to promote your personal brand or your business. The trick is you need to do it subtly. Adding an advertisement to your answer can cause you problems such as having your answer removed from viewing.

One way to promote yourself or your cause is in crafting your credentials. Your credentials are posted at the top of every answer you provide. You can have multiple credentials you can draw from to answer a specific question and to raise your credibility and on-line exposure.

Here are examples of credentials I use regularly:

Rae A. Stonehouse RN Author, Writer & Speaker

40+ years as an RN. Not an expert, but certainly experienced!

Serial Entrepreneur: Until I make some money, I eat a lot of cereal!

40+ years as RN in Mental Health & Graduate of the School of Hard Knocks!

Self-promoter "Blow Your Own Horn!" If you don't, who will?

Author of E=Emcee Squared: Tips & Techniques to Becoming a Dynamic Emcee.

I have a collection of 37 or so of them, so far, I can use as the need arises.

When you answer a question in an area you want to promote yourself in, you can add links to resource material you have created.

Another way can be to say something like "In my business as a website developer I have found... You can find some free resources at my site."

As an author, you can create and upload your Bio. I use the one I currently use as an author i.e. Rae A. Stonehouse RN Author, Writer & Speaker. I have included it elsewhere in this book, so I won't post it here.

Consistency is important when posting your Bio, as people may discover it in different locations on-line.

Your Bio and many of your answers on Quora may be indexed by search engines. I don't know what they use as a criteria for which questions and answers they list and those they don't. Perhaps the number of answer views or Likes triggers a listing?

I only answer questions that resonate with me and I feel I have something to add to the discussion. If I see a question has been adequately answered by others, I won't spend the time trying to come up with something new unless of course I have a completely different perspective worth forwarding.

If you are a creative content developer as I am, there is value in repurposing the content you have created.

I have copied many of my answers and then shared them on my social media venues, i.e. Facebook and Linkedin. I have also posted them as blogs on my different websites related to a particular topic. For example, an answer on business networking could be posted on 3 or 4 different websites I own. I have also added some of my Quora answers to my self-help books, where I believe they can add to the discussion or understanding of a subject. You will find some posted in the Resource Section of this book as examples.

Yes, it is a lot of work. I tend to do bulk uploads to the sites and back date the entries to the original posting on Quora.

The advantage to undertaking all this work is that many of your original Quora posts and your website blog entries will be indexed by search engines, which in turn will draw traffic to your website and help promote you.

Like any other self-promoting/marketing activity, it does take time and effort. While I check Quora at least once a day, I have been coasting for the last year in only answering the occasional question as I have been focusing on writing books and creating on-line courses. There are only so many hours in a day...

IN THE NEXT CHAPTER WE LOOK AT REDDIT, YET ANOTHER SOCIAL media venue that may be of benefit in self-promoting.

REDDIT

Reddit

Reddit refers to itself as the self-styled "front page of the Internet."

According to their on-line promo, "The most important part of Reddit is the sharing."

"Without users sharing links and information and stories and stuff with each other, there'd be no Reddit at all. So, the best way to acquaint yourself with the community is to throw yourself into the mix of things: leave comments, post things you find interesting/cool/horrible/strange, and 'upvote' and 'downvote'" things."

"Oh, hold on, real quick—upvoting and downvoting is how Reddit democracy works. You vote an item up in the ranking or you vote it down. Pretty easy. There are some algorithms that go with the number (the score) you see next to each item, which is apparently time travel-y, but we don't need to get into that today. For now, just know that if you like something, upvote it, and if you don't like something, downvote it."

1.1 So what is Reddit?

Reddit is a social bookmarking website with more than 170,000,000 unique visitors each month that allows you to submit links (or text with links) pointing to various web pages and resources like images, videos, blog articles or just ideas and thoughts. Once submitted, people can upvote or downvote your link, write comments, ask questions and generally interact with whatever you're trying to show them.

1.2 Reddit's Structure - What are the Sub-Reddits?

Reddit is divided into categories called sub-reddits, each of which has a topic and usually its own niche community of people interested in it. For example, the second most popular sub-reddit is called AdviceAnimals (~4 million subscribers) and is targeted towards animal lovers. Another similar but more-targeted sub-reddit is the cats one (~200,000 subscribers).

When you first enter Reddit, you are presented with a list of popular links from different sub-reddits that you are subscribed to by default - usually the biggest and most general ones. This is called The Front Page and is a syndication of the most upvoted and commented links.

Each sub-reddit is essentially a page on its own with unique content, branding, rules and audience.

1.3 Creating an Account on Reddit

Using Reddit is all about content submission and upvoting. In order to submit a link you'll need to create an account, but don't worry - it takes only a minute and an email confirmation is not required.

It's generally a good idea to verify your account nevertheless, since if you ever forget your password there'll be no other way to retrieve a new one.

1.4 Subscribing to and using Sub-Reddits

Once you are logged in, the first thing you'll see is a slightly different Front Page. On the left you see a panel with few tabs, the 'Subscribed' one highlighted by default – that's your default front page with all the sub-reddits you're subscribed to by default. In order to unsubscribe, click the EDIT link at the top right corner to see a full list with all the sub-reddits and your own list of subscriptions.

1.5 Adding Friends on Reddit

Reddit is a social community, so it's pretty normal to be able to add friends to your account and actually following their posting and commenting. Adding friends is easy - just go to Preferences -> Friends, from there you can add, delete and view a list of all your friends.

Source: http://www.redditsecrets.com/how-to-use-reddit-tutorial

Final Thoughts on Reddit:

I created a Reddit account a couple years ago to market my **You're Hired! Job Search Strategies That Work** series of books.

I joined a couple groups related to job searching and other elements of the job interviewing process. I answered a few questions on those subjects, however, with other projects on the go, I haven't visited there for a while.

I'll have to add visit Reddit to my To Do List.

My son swears by Reddit. His passion is history and politics and says he uses Reddit every day to see what is going on in the world.

One thing that jumps out at me is it seems many people are posting information a little too subjective or revealing. Posting personal or confidential information about someone you know can't be a good idea. The on-line world can be very small at times, and what you post can come back to give you grief.

Reddit can be a good source of information on subjects you are interested in. As a self-promoter, being active in providing assistance to others can go a long way in helping you become recognized as an influencer and increase your global reach.

In the next chapter we look at webinars as a way to promote yourself.

WEBINARS

I subscribe to quite a few marketing, sales & social media related newsletters that are delivered to my e-mail inbox on a regular basis.

I have noticed there is frequently a link to an on-line webinar the business has created to feature or explain at length, some aspect of their business.

Often there is an invitation to participate in a live webinar or to view a recording of the event at your convenience. The webinar platforms have improved quite a bit over the past couple of years, to the point that the recordings they create are excellent quality.

There are quite a few webinar platforms to choose from. Most, if not all, offer the following features:

- Two way live video & audio streaming (you are able to see & hear the presenters and selected participants)
- Ability to record the session
- Presenter screen sharing (some allow participants to share their screen)
- Live Chat via texting

- Whiteboard (ability to draw on a screen and share the contents)
- File sharing
- Screen Sharing
- On-line polling

There are an increasing amount of webinar platforms for you to choose from. There are free versions available that might meet your needs. The paid versions might be out of reach for your budget, however, piggybacking off of someone who has a webinar platform account for their business might be an option.

On the other hand, having your own webinar account would allow you to brand your recorded webinars.

When you are assessing and deciding which webinar platform to use, it is important to keep ease of use in mind for both you and your expected participants. Bells and whistles for features are fun to think about, but if they are not accessible for everyone involved, they are of little value.

I have found that the browser-based webinar platforms seem to be the easiest to work with. Asking your participants to download software onto their computer before they can participate can be logistically challenging for them as well as raise suspicion in many people.

Browser-based platforms will likely request that the participant download a small piece of software that easily installs and is supposed to delete itself when you leave the program. Not being a techie, I am unable to attest to that fact though.

An 'evergreen' webinar i.e. where the information isn't time dated or becomes redundant can be a good way to promote your business. By recording your webinar, you can then post it to Facebook or your YouTube channel.

There is some disagreement whether your webinar should be recorded with a live audience vs just you delivering the presentation without an audience. You could try either method and see how your results are.

In our next chapter, I finally end this book and offer a summary and concluding thoughts.

∼

"Resolve to be a master of change rather than a victim of change." Brian Tracy

"A feeling of confidence and personal power comes from facing challenges and overcoming them." Brian Tracy

SUMMARY & CONCLUSION

Final Thoughts on Self-Promotion

Self-promotion is probably as much a mind-set as it is a set of strategies.

You need to believe in yourself. You need to believe you are just as good as anybody else. And you have to believe you are worthy of success.

I would like to conclude with an article from Search Engine Journal on the 10 Essential elements to Create & Sustain Brand Identity. While written from a business perspective, the suggestions apply to individual business professionals as well.

It all begins with building a strong brand identity. An element that includes not just logos or taglines, but every form of communication or business strategy.

The mission doesn't stop there. Once you achieve a strong brand identity, you must sustain it.

You can't create a strong brand identity through a cookie-cutter process. Every business or personal journey will need to be personalized.

With that said, though, a few essential elements are required, which are listed below.

1. Find & Focus on Your Target Audience

Firstly, understand your intended audience.

Know their passions, goals, decision-making processes – basically whatever is needed to speak directly to them in the most fluent way.

The same goes for building your brand identity. Once you know who you are speaking to, you can adjust your brand-building tactics to reflect that audience's needs and make a larger impact.

If your business sells health products for animals, you must first know who your customers are – from their frustrations (my cat doesn't swallow pills!) to when they're most actively thinking about their pet health to how they interact with other health products on the market (quick social media search makes this easy).

Find that target audience by researching competitors and what questions are being asked across social channels like Quora, Medium, Reddit and the typical outlets like Facebook and Twitter.

Next, build a persona file by asking and outlining the following of your target audience:

- What are their goals?
- What are their frustrations?
- What prompts their decisions to act?
- How do they interact with other brands and their services/products?

With that persona in mind, begin building your brand identity around them. What mediums does the target audience favor? Video or personal interaction with other users of the product/services?

Or, if an author, does the target audience mostly read the actual books, or absorb the book through what others think of that author?

These questions and answers can shape everything from your website's design to your social interaction to your personality to your writing style.

It's easier to market to a target audience versus everyone. Find them and tailor your conversation for them.

2. Create a Unique Selling Proposition

What makes you different? Or as Seth Godin says, what makes you "remarkable?"

In simplest terms, the answer is your unique selling position, or USP.

Here is where a major problem occurs when attempting to create a strong brand identity. Many people immediately study the businesses or individuals who have the largest market share and popularity and intimidate those top players.

What makes you different? Or what can you do to differentiate yourself from the others?

This principle needs to be reiterated over and over throughout the business or personal adventure, and it becomes part of the fabric of your USP and, eventually, your brand identity.

Spend much time on this and make it an essential element to exploit when building your brand identity.

3. Expose Your Core Values – But Remember They're Built on Perceptions

Exposing your core values is another essential element when creating your brand identity. For a personal brand, such as a self-development guru or fiction author, it's easy to guide the perception of values.

Based on some quick perceptions, it's easy to see that Tony Robbins is out to change the world to a more positive place. And Edward

Snowden wanted to change the worldview of politicals and government by becoming a whistleblower.

For a business, though, guiding perceptions is not so easy. And the bigger the organization, the tougher the process.

If one employee's core values are unethical and out of line, and that employee does something drastic, he or she can quickly take down an entire business.

Like a USP, exposing your core values is not easy work – especially because your brand is built upon perceptions.

The ultimate reason to highlight your core values? If others share similar values, you'll build a fan base quicker.

As Howard Schultz says, "If people believe they share values with a company, they will stay loyal to the brand."

4. Unique Personality

When you have worked on creating your USP and combine it with your core values, your personality surfaces.

Is your personality passion-driven? Are you tech-forward in search of making the laborious task simple? Or is your brand highlighted by exposing the social talk around a certain subject?

Whether you like it or not, your personality is part of your brand identity. Remember this when building yours. For personal ventures, incorporating your personality is simpler because one voice exists.

But, just like values explained in the point above, when a business is involved – and many people help create that brand image – multiple personalities mix. This can result in a brand identity that may appear bipolar if not thought out.

Make sure everyone included within the company understands the personality that needs to be presented the same way across the company, from the salespeople to the marketing department to the CEO's interactions with the public.

5. Consistency Across Every Channel

When creating and building your brand identity, keep your messaging and voice consistent across every channel of communication.

The social media channels are obvious but don't forget your blogs, guest blogs, website copy, PR efforts, newsletters, email replies, paid advertising copy or conversations with everyone that you come in contact with.

Remember, also, that consistency across every channel is vital not only while creating but also while sustaining your brand identity.

6. No Me, Me, Me Talk; Be Genuine and Add Endless Value

This is one of the most annoying byproducts of many people when they begin building their brand – especially those who hit it big quickly. I call it the "me, me, me" talk.

When you see communication channels of a business or individual that only exploits what they have accomplished or what they offer, it robs any focus on the reader. These me, me, me talks don't offer value to would-be fans of the brand, and dilutes any value that the brand intends to deliver.

Smaller businesses are notorious for this because they typically look at their biggest perceived competitor and mimic what that competitor is doing.

Past accomplishments are an essential element to building a strong brand identity, but it shouldn't be the focus. When a brand brags about their accomplishments, it's a sign they are stuck in the past.

The brands that will garner the most brand identity strength are those that offer innovative services/products and communicate with a focus on the future over the past.

7. Focus on Positives

Zig Ziglar says, "Positive thinking will let you do everything better than negative thinking will."

The same concept goes for focusing on the positives over the negatives within your industry. People naturally attract optimistic thinkers – especially those who have proven they're genuine over "me, me, me" talkers.

If your brand – personal or business – is living through a super down period in your respective industry, don't focus on the negatives. Rather, focus on the positives. Show your perseverance for forward-looking thinking, and you'll naturally attract a following.

Leave the negative criticism to the news writers. Focus on the positive future as Warren Buffett focuses on his stock picks – he remains upbeat by purchasing with enthusiasm during the downbeat market, and he continues to win.

8. Make Promises & Stick To Them

Those with the most powerful brand identity constantly make promises and stick to them.

From people like Steve Jobs who was out to change the world of personal computing to Starbuck's position on improving education by offering school to part-time workers, these well-known brands make promises and stick with them.

Learn from these greats. If you can keep a promise, people will associate your brand with authenticity. And authenticity streamlines loyalty, turning customers/clients/patients/readers into fans.

9. Extend Your Brand at Every Opportunity

Your brand identity is mostly created through your communications, from your social presence to logos to website colors to how you speak to the media.

But other opportunities exist to extend your brand. A few I've witnessed and mimicked were:

Email signatures that highlight your most valuable blog work.

Business cards that are slightly different in design and feature a tagline.

Even slides that differ from the majority during a presentation.

Think of every single area where you are represented and extend your brand to that area.

10. Don't Forget to Evolve

Don't become stagnant. As the world changes, the strongest brands change with it.

Some, like Apple and Tesla, evolve due to rapid technology changes. But then again, they make an underlying promise to always adapt and deliver the very best products using the latest in technology.

Regardless of how some of the world's most known brands changed, one thing typically remained – the core values of those brands. These are typically deep rooted and authentic, and when they shift people lose interest.

Source: https://www.searchenginejournal.com/brand-identity/343941/#close

WHILE I'M A FIRM BELIEVER IN SELF-PROMOTION, I BALANCE IT with not taking myself too seriously.

If you are interested, check out my personal website at raestonehouse.com. It starts off with 'Welcome to the Wonderful World of Rae Stonehouse! 50 Shades of Rae, if you will!'

The *promotional copy* goes on to say, 'Over the years of entrepreneurial pursuits I have learned the value of self-promotion.

While I have learned that you can't control what anybody else writes about you, yes Trolls are still among us, you can make it easy for someone who really wants to learn more about you.

This website is designed to provide you with more than you probably ever wanted to know about me... and some!

I also believe that I am a creator of valuable content that should be shared. As a graduate of the School of Hard Knocks, my passion is in creating self-help articles in the category of "Tips & Techniques to..."

You will find an ever-increasing collection of articles that will be of value to you.

In some ways, it is very much a scrapbook of interests and issues important to me.

In the next and final section of this book, I offer resource files you can read to see a different perspective on many of the topics we have covered.

PART V
NETWORKING RESOURCE FILES

STRATEGIES TO GET THE MOST OUT OF YOUR BUSINESS NETWORKING/REFERRAL GROUP

You have done your research and decided upon a referral group that works for you. So now what? How do you get value out of your membership?

Strategy One: Develop your 30-second to one minute elevator pitch. Most groups will allow you that much time to promote yourself. Practice saying it out loud, even to family members or the family pet if they will listen. The intent is you become comfortable saying it without getting nervous. This will go a long way in reducing the performance anxiety that often accompanies shyness.

Strategy Two: Practice saying your name out loud and the name of your business. If you haven't developed your USP (Universal Sales Proposition) now is the time to do so.

Strategy Three: For your fellow group members to be able to promote your business, you need to teach them exactly what it is you do or have to offer. If the group offers a member showcase as part of the meeting, i.e. where members have an allotted amount of time to present to the group, get yourself on the speaking schedule. Prepare and practice a presentation that introduces yourself to the group.

Subsequent presentations can allow you to demonstrate your expertise or knowledge on a particular subject.

Strategy Four: Obtain a membership list for your group and send a postcard or thank you note to all the members of the group thanking them for allowing you to join them. It is a great way to plug your business and offer your services to your fellow members.

Strategy Five: Develop a plan to go out for 'coffee talk' with each of your fellow members to get to know them better and to share with them what your business is all about.

Strategy Six: If you are finding the networking in your club to be too challenging and out of your comfort zone, consider asking one of your fellow members to mentor you. Some people seem to be natural networkers, but in fact they are highly skilled. If they can do it, you can too!

Strategy Seven: As a member, you are expected to help build the club. Invite your fellow business colleagues out to a meeting. If you are already a friend of theirs, it can help leverage your reach with your fellow members.

Strategy Eight: Some groups tend to sit down at tables as soon as they arrive in the meeting room. Arrive five to ten minutes before the meeting starts and plan on staying an extra five or so at the end. It can be a great way to have a quick conversation with a member that you haven't had the chance to get to know very well yet.

Strategy Nine: Try to sit across or beside someone different at each meeting. Again, a great way to get to know your fellow members in a social setting.

Strategy Ten: Befriend a guest. This can be a good way to meet a potential business connection in a safe setting. Even if they don't join your group, you can still develop a relationship with them.

Strategy Eleven: Once you are comfortable with the group consider taking on a leadership role. Serving as a 'servant leader' can help develop your influence, which can help develop your reputation as the 'one to go to' for help.

Probably one of the biggest challenges that members face is that they don't see results as fast as they would like to. It takes time to build relationships. People like to do business with people that they trust. Learning to trust people and becoming a person that others trust may take a while.

~

NAME DROPPING FOR FUN & PROFIT

Does this sound familiar? You are at a business networking session and you are captivated by a speaker who wants to regale you with a litany of important people they have supposedly recently spent time with. "Oh, the other day I had coffee with the Mayor..." "I was just saying the very same thing to my good friend XXX, you know he owns half the town." "Yeah, my best friend is the Crown Attorney, and she was telling me..."

To coin a phrase... "blah, blah, blah, yaddey, yaddey, yaddey!"

I suppose it is a fact of life we need to accept. There are some people in life who need to name drop to build up their ego or their sense of importance. On the other hand, I have met some people who are so narcissistic it would never occur to them that their listener doesn't know the individuals they have offered as proof of something, nor would even care if they did know them.

Having worked in mental health/psychiatry for 40+ years, I have learned at least one concept that has served me well and that is "all behaviour has meaning." The challenge is we don't often know what the meaning is or what purpose it is serving, and likely the other individual doesn't either.

A person who has a tendency to drop names of important people into conversation, and the term "important" is subjective, could be nervous or lack self-confidence in a 1-1 conversation.

Talking about "important" people could be a maladaptive coping mechanism, one to relieve the individual's anxiety. If the person they are talking about is well known or popular, the concept seems to be some of that popularity will rub off on them. It is probably similar to bragging about one's self.

Once you recognize the individual is monopolizing the conversation and playing a game of "look who I know!" what do you do about it?

Not taking action is one choice. You could continue to listen to the one-sided conversation. Odds are if they have dropped some names into conversation they likely have quite a few more to offer. It would probably be a good idea to extricate yourself by excusing yourself before you doze off.

Another option could be to derail the conversation i.e. take it off its likely track by saying something to the effect of "Oh you know XXX. I have been wanting to meet them for a while. Could you introduce us or arrange a meeting?"

This action on your part could have a positive outcome if the individual actually does know the V.I.P. and can introduce you to them. Or if they don't really know them, they may start to back paddle i.e. change the topic or avoid the request made of them and keep the conversation going in a direction where they continue to own it.

A third option could be a variation of the old "See you later, alligator!" At a business networking function odds are high you can leave this one-sided conversation and move on to a more productive one.

Is there a time when it is appropriate for *you* to name drop? Yes, I believe so. Name dropping or inserting another person's name into the conversation can help build your credibility as someone who is well-connected, one who has a good understanding on a particular topic and it can even develop your personal influence.

Some examples might be:

- When having a conversation about a particular topic, issue or problem and you know someone who has faced a similar situation, you could mention their name and describe the lessons they learned as they dealt with the subject.
- You could offer your services as an intermediary and propose to introduce the person you are speaking with to someone who you know who could be in a position to assist them.
- At a later date, perhaps at a "getting to know you" coffee meeting you could explore with each other who each of you knows and if there is a possibility any of these connections could be of value in helping with a current need.

I hope through this article I have been able to raise your awareness to the "name-dropper" style of networker and offer you some ideas on how to deal with them. But then again... name dropping can be an effective networking tool if used effectively. Try it out and see how it works for you. Even better still... become one of those people who other people fit into their conversations.

CLOSE ENCOUNTERS OF THE NETWORKING KIND

Have you ever wondered how close to stand to another person when conversing in a 1 to 1 at a business networking session? Okay, maybe I do have too much spare time as they say, but I am sure this is a question many people have asked.

While I don't have a definitive answer, I do have some thoughts on the matter. Many factors including gender, culture, trust, past experiences and self-confidence come into play.

Looking at it from a self-defense, self-preservation perspective, it is helpful to think of each of us having an invisible circle or a safety zone around us. As a preservation measure, we tend to keep strangers outside of our safety zone and only let people we trust or are comfortable with into our comfort zone.

In North America, our personal safety zone tends to be about three feet in diameter around us. The same distance as our outstretched arm and fist or our outstretched leg if we were intending to strike or kick someone in self-defense. Our comfort zone, i.e. the area where we will let those we trust, tends to be about 18 to 30 inches in diameter.

In a business networking session, I'm sure we don't attend with the idea we are going to have to physically defend ourselves. However, I believe this is a situation that can cause stress in some people in networking situations. To have an effective discussion with someone who you are meeting for the first time as in a business networking session often means you are permitting a stranger to enter your comfort zone. Crowded, noisy rooms tend to necessitate drawing in closer to the other person just to be able to hear them well.

While it's socially acceptable for women to hold or touch each other while in conversation, even in a first meeting encounter, the same cannot be said about two men conversing.

You may not even be aware you have a comfort zone until someone invades it. That feeling of anxiousness, uneasiness may be your subconscious calling to your attention something isn't right. Perhaps it is the time to take a step backwards to continue your conversation.

If you are confident in your networking conversations, allowing others into your comfort zone and paying close attention to the conversation by actively participating in it can go a long way in building your reputation as an effective networker and somebody worth meeting and getting to know.

Many networkers have challenges of inserting themselves into groups that have already formed and are actively discussing a topic. A group where the members are standing close enough to converse with each other, yet not within each other's comfort zones, would likely be a group open to having someone else join them.

On the other hand, two people standing very close together, perhaps a little ways away from the rest of the group would seem to be having an intimate conversation and would not likely be open to someone joining them. If they were to separate from each other it could indicate the private or intimate stage of their conversation has concluded and they were now open to be joined by others.

You can learn a lot be observing others. In your next networking session observe how people are standing. Are they close together or far apart? Does an individual networker use the same technique with everyone they meet or do they vary their closeness in conversation? Try out some different distances to your conversational partner and see how it feels to you.

FOR A GOOD TIME CALL

I am sure most of us have heard of the practice of reading a message scrawled on a public restroom wall of "For a good time call..." There is a usually a phone number accompanying the message. In all likelihood the individual mentioned is not aware of the advertising being done on their behalf, nor would they likely agree with it. More than likely it was scrawled by an adolescent male, driven by testosterone and thinking it was pretty funny. Having not spent any time in the women's restroom, I can only assume this practice only happens in the men's.

If the individual named actually wrote the message in question, well I guess it could be attributed to some savvy targeted marketing.

I'm not suggesting you add this to your networking skills repertoire. In my example the call for action is *"for a good time call..."* Each and everyone of us has something we are offering, whether it be a skill or our expertise. When we are networking for business, we need to get the message out there as to what we do and what we have to offer.

Now, using a plumber as an example, what if we changed the message to something like for "For No More Leaky Pipes call..." A financial planner might say "We are your financial health experts. Will your money live as long as you do?" An entertainer could get away with "for a good time call..."

This in essence is your USP, which is often defined as Universal Sale Pitch or Unique Selling Proposition. Your USP is a short statement that summarizes who you are, what you do, why you are passionate about it and how you are different or better than anyone else who does it. All this in a short sentence. Yes, it is definitely challenging. You may not want to do it, but your competition likely is.

A memorable USP has a way of connecting you, your business and what you have to offer in a person's mind. You want your potential customer to automatically think of you when they have a problem to solve and that you are likely the solution to it. The only way it will happen is you have to get in the habit of using your USP regularly, perhaps as part of your elevator pitch. You have to become known by your USP.

At the risk of self-promoting, after all I am an entrepreneur, I would offer one of my USPs. "Hi, I'm Rae Stonehouse also known as Mr. Emcee. I am on Okanagan-based full service master of ceremonies and event planner. From start to finish... we do it all!"

Or... for a good time call Rae... just not too early in the morning, too late in the evening, on weekends or in the afternoon as it cuts into my nap. But other than that...

JOHNNY APPLESEED KNEW WHAT HE WAS DOING

Legend has it that Johnny Appleseed traveled the American countryside spreading apple seeds randomly everywhere he went.

In fact, according to Wikipedia, he planted nurseries rather than orchards, built fences around them to protect them from livestock, left the nurseries in the care of a neighbor who sold trees on shares, and returned every year or two to tend the nursery.

Many people's business networking activities can be a lot like randomly spreading those apple seeds. Some might grow, but most likely left to their own, they will fail to develop and eventually die off.

Relationships need to be nurtured. Often the word *cultivated* is used to describe what needs to take place for a relationship to grow. Both words are really describing an active interest, desire and taking action oriented steps to develop a relationship with another individual.

So how does one *cultivate* a relationship? I have some cynical colleagues who would say that would treat them the same way as you would cultivate mushrooms. You keep them in the dark and feed them BS [male cow manure.] I would suspect they have few quality connections. I certainly wouldn't want to be connected to them with that attitude.

Let's leave the agriculture analogy for a while and go to back to the question of how does one cultivate a relationship?

Consider these following steps or actions: (They aren't necessarily in the order you would take. Relationship building can be more of a circuitous journey rather than a lineal one.)

- Research the individual. Check them out on Linkedin. Find out what their vocation and background is.
- Invite them out for coffee. Look for common interests.
- Be on the lookout for resource materials related to their interests and forward it on to them.
- Send them thank-you notes or appropriate gifts to recognize help they have provided to you.
- Send congratulatory messages e.g. cards/notes by snail mail or perhaps by e-mail for important milestones both personal and business. Seeing their name in the paper can be a great opportunity to drop them a note and congratulate them, assuming it wasn't in Crime Stoppers or the Most Wanted List of course.
- If you are comfortable in doing so, send them business referrals. The Law of Reciprocity says if you do something good for somebody else they in turn will do something good for you.
- Perhaps you have heard of the concept of "unconditional love?" To successfully cultivate a relationship you can't put terms in place. Doing so could jeopardize the relationship.
- Don't appear to be a stalker with your focused interest.

So far we have been looking at *active* steps you can take. For a relationship to develop, you have to be open to sharing of yourself. It can't be a one way transaction. There has to be a payoff for you as well.

Getting back to my agricultural analogy of cultivating, sometimes you have to do some pruning to help strengthen your plantings. The same thing applies to your network. There will always be people who are suspicious of your motives or intentions. Perhaps this isn't somebody you want in your network.

There will also be people who, once you get to know them, you find you really don't want to associate with them. It might be necessary to sever all ties with the individual. If you aren't comfortable dealing with or relating to an individual, you are unlikely to want to refer them to another connection. Their behaviour could have the undesirable affect of reflecting on you and your business.

An interesting side note mentioned in the Wikipedia article stated that apple trees grown from seed are rarely sweet or tasty, more on the sour side, which was apparently perfect for producing hard cider and applejack back in those days. Modern day orchardists plant strains of trees that consistently produce a fruit that is desirable and marketable. There is no use in providing all the labor in cultivating a crop if you aren't able to realize a bountiful harvest.

So when it comes to business networking, will you randomly toss out those seeds or will you take your time and cultivate a manageable amount of productive connections? Your choice... sweet or sour?

SO WHAT'S YOUR STORY?

"Nice day eh?"
"Too bad about the Canucks!"
"Isn't this weather something?"

We have heard them all before... meaningless comments more likely to end a conversation than to advance it.

FOR THE MANY PEOPLE WE ENCOUNTER DURING OUR DAILY TRAVELS, perhaps this is all that is needed. If we had long drawn out conversations with everyone, we likely wouldn't accomplish everything we need to in a day.

However, attending and getting the most out of a business networking session is another story [pun intended]. This is the perfect opportunity for you to share your success stories. A success story is a short, punchy anecdote. It teaches your conversation partner about your business, what you are interested in, and hopefully gives the listener a reason to get to know you better. All that in about 2 to 3 minutes!

This concept was reinforced to me recently when I attended a local

Chamber of Commerce event. A fellow networker asked me how my society was going. At the time I was the Chairman for a local entrepreneur society. I went into my spiel of the challenges we were facing in moving forward. One step forward, two steps backwards.

I realized later I had missed a perfect opportunity to promote the volunteer opportunities available within the society, as well as the opportunity to share my vision for the future of the society. I had invested a lot of time and energy in moving the society forward and I should have been prepared to share the story with whoever was willing to hear it.

It is often said that misery loves company. Does your present conversational companion really want to share your misery? I have met far too many people over the years whose default mode is what I call "poor pitiful me."

I recognize it readily, having used it myself in my early years. Many people find it easier to share with others how awful life is treating them rather than sharing success stories. The logical conclusion would be if you were coming from a position of self-pity, then you are unlikely to have a collection of success stories.

Many of our mothers have taught us not to talk about ourselves. "Nobody likes braggers!" Walt Whitman is quoted as saying "If you done it, it ain't bragging." While not grammatically correct, it is the essence of sharing your story.

Each of us has multiple personas based on the different roles we have in life. Some describe it "as wearing many hats." We may be at a business networking session to market our business but we still have our different personas with us at all times and we should be prepared to share a success story related to any of those personas if the opportunity arises.

As in many endeavors, the key to success is advance preparation. Take stock of what is new and exciting in your life that others would appreciate hearing about. Share your enthusiasm!

So how does one create a good story? You would think the answer would be to start at the beginning, but you would be wrong. I would suggest that start creating your story by developing the ending first.

What do you hope to achieve by sharing a story? Are you hoping someone will follow you in your cause? Will you be educating somebody on a topic or issue of importance to you, or is your intention merely to entertain? The most important part to remember with developing your conclusion to your story is "What do you want the listener to take away from your story?"

With your "take away" clearly in your mind, you can now carry on to developing your opening for your story. This is the part where you want to grab your listener's attention so they are eager to listen to the rest of your story.

Using fishing with a rod as an analogy, your story's opening is the bait you are using to attract the fish to bite. The content of your story being the moving the rod up and down, praying for a bite. Setting the hook and landing the fish being the conclusion of your story.

I left out the part about drinking a lot of beer as I recall from my long-ago days of fishing. Your story's opening should be short and to the point, yet be teasing enough for the listener to want to hear more.

A: "So what's new?"

B: "Not much, same ole, same ole. How about you?"

A: "The same. Business sucks. Can't make a decent living in this economy."

B: "We'll catch you later on the flip side."

A: "Okay, see ya."

Does this sound familiar? "A" set up the discussion with "So what's new?" "B" missed the opportunity to share a story about what is new and exciting in their life. Neither gained anything from this interaction.

You are at a business networking event and you are asked the very same question "So what's new?" Now what do you do? It's story time! If you have had previous conversations with this individual on a particular subject, I would suggest updating them on anything new with the same subject.

If you haven't had a previous conversation with your fellow networker, the field is wide open. You can talk about what's new and exciting about your business. Often there is an awkward period just after two networkers have introduced themselves to each other and delivered their elevator pitches.

If they haven't found common areas of interest, there can be a lull while each rapidly thinks of where to take the conversation. Instead of waiting for the "What's new" question, you could interject into the conversation and take it in a different direction. Yours!

So what's new? Go ahead... ask me!

"I've been working as a registered nurse for over 40 years and having worked with thousands of people over the years I thought I had seen everything. The other day I..."

"As a master organizer, I help organizations create events that raise attention for their cause as well as much needed funds. One of my clients was pleasantly surprised when I ..."

"Our entrepreneurs society helps create entrepreneurial leaders. We have a young woman working with us who has done some amazing things for us..."

"One of the things in life I'm passionate about is in honing my communication and leadership skills. I've been a member of Toastmasters for almost 25 years and continue to learn something new. The other day I learned..."

"I've been doing a lot of writing lately. One project is a series of articles related to business networking entitled "Is Your Net Working." My latest one is about..."

So... what's your story?

BLOW YOUR OWN HORN!

TOO SHY TO NETWORK?

"Do your hands start sweating and your legs shake with the thought of having to not only attend a business networking session but actually talk to people?"

"Do you feel paralyzed by the fear of rejection when you are at a business networking event?

"Would you rather have a root canal than attend a business networking event?

"Would you rather send an e-mail to a business lead than meet them in person?"

Well, if any of these apply... you may be shy!

"Get over it!" That's what our extroverted friends would say. "Just do what we do!"

Life isn't that simple. We aren't all extroverts, and it would probably be a noisy world if we were. Being shy isn't a personal defect.

You aren't the only one out there, even if it feels like it sometimes. The world is full of shy people and it *doesn't* prevent you from being an effective networker and *reaping the benefits* networking can bring to your business.

Shyness can be defined as a reticence and self-consciousness, not just in stressful social situations but over all.

Studies in shyness back in 1972 at Stanford University's Shyness Clinic indicated that 40% of Americans considered themselves to be shy. Nowadays, closer to 50% are likely to say that they are shy. You would think with all the advancements in modern sciences and the humanities we would become more outgoing. Perhaps all those advances are what are causing us to become shyer.

It has been said it started with ATMs and Walkmans. We are no longer obligated to stand in line at our financial institutions to do our banking. We can do it with a machine. The opportunity to talk to your neighbor while standing in line is lost as well as small talk with the teller.

Grocery stores and many other ones now have self-checkouts. No need to interact with a check-out clerk anymore. Walkmans allowed us to walk and listen to our music, for our ears only, a great way to escape unwanted conversations. The Walkman developed into MP3 players and smart phones, while getting smaller have offered us more ways to escape the real world.

The traditional family is no longer traditional. The days where the father went to work, the mother stayed home and the children went to school, all to come home at the end of the day to share a meal and their adventures of the day only exists in reruns of Leave it to Beaver.

Traditional meals were replaced by TV dinners, then microwaveable ones. Fast food has become even faster and arguably not even food anymore. The opportunity to develop one's communication and conversing skills around the family dinner table may be lost forever.

I believe you can place the condition of shyness on a continuum. On one end you would have an individual who is painfully shy. The mere thought of having to go to a networking event and conversing with people could be enough to cause them to have a panic attack. Any situation where one feels that they are likely to die is to be avoided at all costs.

At the other end of continuum would be someone who experiences some mild apprehension about participating in networking events. They feel the apprehension but do it anyway.

So how do we move upwards on the continuum to the point where we are less apprehensive about meeting and socializing with people, even to the point of enjoying it?

As a registered nurse working most of my career in mental health, I realize there will be some individuals who will only be able to move forward by taking an anti-anxiety medication such as lorazepam to reduce their anxiety. This is only recommended for those who have severe difficulty and only for the short term.

Despite what some physicians will say, these medications are only to be used for short durations. Coming off of the medication can be as stressful for the person as the situation the medication was taken for in the first place.

I believe the secret to becoming more social i.e. moving away from shy is a cognitive behavioral one combined with skill development. There are a few clinical modalities that might be of use. Some might say it is not important to know why you are shy or what causes your symptoms.

"Forget about it, move forward, do it anyways!" A *Reality Therapy* approach might be "You are shy because you choose to be. What are you going to do to change it and become more social?"

A *Solutions Focused* approach would likely say something like "Tell me what it would look like if you were no longer shy. What would you be doing? Who would you be talking to? What would you be saying to them? How would you be feeling?" They wouldn't be focusing on the past, only on how the future *could be*.

I'm a proponent of the Solutions Focused Method combined with education and experience.

There are many parallels with the fear of public speaking and shyness in social situations. Over the past 25 years I have been honing my public speaking skills by studying public speaking as a member of Toastmasters. Both within my club with fellow members and out in the public, I regularly challenge myself by delivering presentations and speeches.

Darren Lacroix, the 2001 World Champion of Public Speaking describes the secret to becoming a better public speaker as being "Stage time, stage time, stage time." I believe the secret to becoming less shy and more self-confident is similar. You need to face your fear of networking by getting out there and doing it, over and over again.

Within the Toastmasters program we develop our skills by continually moving forward in our educational program and raising the bar as they say in increasing the challenges we face. The more we speak in public, the more we desensitize ourselves and reduce the power anxiety has over us. The Toastmaster's program also offers constructive feedback as a way to maximize our self-development.

An overall plan to reduce shyness and increase self-confidence would be to include joining Toastmasters. Membership will provide you plenty of opportunities to both develop your communication and leadership skills, but also plenty of opportunities to network in social situations.

Research the topic of business networking. You will find while there are lots written about the subject, finding practical tips and techniques can be challenging to find.

Look for networking events in your community. Don't expect to be a *power networker* from the beginning. As they say you, can't expect to run before you can walk. Learn what you can about the organization facilitating the event. What type of people attend the events? Is it purely social in nature or are people expecting to network for business opportunities?

If you are shy and it is important you network, accompany a friend to the next business networking event, preferably someone who is a little more outgoing than you are. Ask them to introduce you to some people who they know that may be of benefit for you to meet.

As I said in the introduction, if almost 50% of people are saying that they are shy, then odds are there will be a high number of shy people at any event. You won't be alone!

"A character is a completely fashioned will." Novalis

"Your personal philosophy is the greatest determining factor in how your life works out." Jim Rohn

"Concentrate on one thing, the most important thing, and stay with it until it's complete." Brian Tracy

YOU GET BACK WHAT YOU GIVE

I recently noticed the often used saying "You Get Back What You Give" written in large letters on a roadside display board at a local church.

Perhaps they are stating the obvious, but then one's base personality of being an optimist or a pessimist might come into play. Do you see the world as one of opportunity or as one of danger and threats?

If you are a believer in the Law of Attraction, you have likely also heard the sayings "you reap what you sow" or "what you think about comes about." Dr. Ivan Misner, Founder of BNI, describes this as the "Givers Gain" principal.

THE LAW OF RECIPROCITY SAYS IF YOU PROVIDE A SERVICE OR FAVOR for another, they will likely feel obligated to return the favor. I have read somewhere it creates a tension in the individual who has received a favor to the extent they feel a discomfort until they have returned the favor and evened the score. This may be at a subconscious level, and they wouldn't even be aware of why they are doing it.

The example above refers to the results that can occur for helping another individual. Sometimes cause and effect aren't related in time. Meaning you can't always see your results, nor can they always be attributed to your actions.

The Law of Attraction would have you believe if you put out something good to the Universe it will respond by having something good return to you. The results you obtain aren't always related to the good you put out though. It could come back to you from a different, perhaps unexpected source.

So what does this have to do with business networking? When you provide assistance or a favor for another individual without the expectation of gain, the Universe will balance it out and you will receive something in return. Providing a business referral to someone in your network could result in multiple referrals back to you.

An easy way to start this in motion is to create and submit a testimonial for someone in your network and submit it to their Linkedin profile under the appropriate heading i.e. where you have worked with them or know of their work. Odds are they will become motivated to submit one in return on your behalf. This action has an added benefit of displaying your name in their profile which is linked to yours. People are curious and frequently read the Linkedin testimonials. A well written one will reflect well on you.

Another easy favor you can do for someone is to *Like* their Facebook page or a specific entry they have made. It helps to give them credibility as well, highlights your name somewhat. The same applies to Linkedin. Post a favorable comment on something an individual has written or click on the *Like* button.

We all have skills and expertise we use every day in our jobs and businesses. What we take for granted might be awe-inspiring in others. Consider doing some pro bono work for others. Doing so can significantly help someone in need and can also give you a warm fuzzy feeling we sometimes crave. You never know what you will receive in return once you set this action in place.

If you know the person well enough and you are comfortable doing so, offer their name as a referral if someone is looking for a service or product they provide.

Whether you believe in the Law of Attraction or not, there is enough anecdotal evidence out there indicating the principal of "Givers Gain" actually works. I would challenge you to test it out and see for yourself. Try it and see what happens. Let me know how your net's working.

∼

BECOME A THOUGHT LEADER

Wikipedia defines a thought leader as being an individual or firm that is recognized as an authority in a specialized field and whose expertise is sought and often rewarded.

Would being recognized as a leader in your field or in your business make a difference to your bottom line? Is it possible for mere mortals, average people like you and I to become thought leaders?

I believe it is not only possible to become a leader in your specific field, but it is within the reach of most of us to do so. With my keen interest in developing my business networking skills, I'm working towards becoming one of those thought leaders. I write about practical networking skills development for shy people as well as those who have some networking skills and want to improve their success rate.

Am I an expert at networking? In theory, yes, in practice, not as much. I write about the subject of networking and shyness because they have caused me problems throughout my life. I've tested the tips & techniques I offer and I know from firsthand experience they work. I also know the lessons I have learned can be very beneficial to others who are experiencing similar difficulties. Recent studies have indicated that over 50% of Americans consider themselves to be shy. That is a huge market awaiting me to become an expert.

My researching the topic of networking has been educational for me in several ways. I have learned I know more than a lot of people on the subject, yet not as much as I could. My anxiety in networking situations has been steadily reducing as I become more educated on the subject and my effectiveness is increasing.

My goal is to become a thought leader on the subject of business networking. I am open to the fame and fortune that will come my way when I do so. It would be nice though if this happened a little sooner rather than later.

Is it really possible to become the thought leader on a subject you are experienced with? Perhaps it might be helpful to replace the word "the" in the previous sentence with an "a." You don't have to be *the* top expert on your subject. You can become one of many and still be an effective thought leader. You also don't have to compete on the world stage. Odds are your local community and its surrounding geography could support you being its top thought leader on a specific subject.

So how does one become a thought leader? I will offer a few suggestions you might want to consider.

To be a thought leader you actually have to give some thought to the subject you want to be an expert in. That sounds rather obvious at first, but I don't believe it is.

Many entrepreneurs and business people are caught up in working *in* their business rather than working *on* their business. Day to day they provide a service or a product in their business without taking the time to think about how to grow their business so they can realize even greater revenue. Becoming a thought leader involves investing in yourself.

I believe it was Brian Tracy who said if you read about a specific subject for one hour a day, in five years you will become a world leading expert on your subject. In essence, he is referring to becoming a thought leader. Thought leaders are well read.

Thought leaders are also well spoken. Many people believe you are born with good public speaking skills or that it is a gift. There is no truth to that belief. Public speaking skills are no different from any other skills. You get better with practice and feedback providing corrective action. If you don't, you won't. It is also a matter of using it or losing it.

To continually develop your public speaking skills you need to consistently work at it. I have been working on honing my communication skills over the past 25 years as a member of Toastmasters International, the world's leading inexpensive provider of communication and leadership skills development. Whether you are an experienced speaker looking for opportunities to speak or a beginning speaker wanting to get over your stage fright, Toastmasters is the place to do so.

Speak well, speak often!

Thought leaders are good writers. The old saying that "the pen is mightier than the sword" readily comes to mind. To be able to influence people and in turn lead them you need to be able to write in a manner that not only grabs the reader's attention it spurs them into taking action. The challenge is in writing, so your message is understood by the reader. The average North American reads at a grade seven level. Your challenge is to write so they can understand it yet not have your material so dumbed down you insult those with higher literacy skills.

On-line bulletin boards, chat rooms and social media venues such as Linkedin have helped level the playing field for those who tend to be on the shy side. You can be as bold as you want to be with your on-line persona.

Linkedin has a relatively new feature where you can follow Thought Leaders from around the world. Some of them like Sir Richard Branson have a couple million followers. I don't follow him, but I guess a lot of people are interested in what he has to say. Others on the list have a mere 30000 followers. Wouldn't that be nice? It helps to look at that 30000 or so as being a number that could be achievable, assuming of course that it is something you desired.

I'm guessing, but I believe Linkedin likely has a group dedicated to almost any subject that you can think of. You are allowed to follow and be a member of up to 50 groups at a time. To help gain exposure for yourself, you can post questions or submit an article of interest to share with others.

You can also provide answers or commentary on questions or discussions others have posted. This can be a great way to create credibility for yourself and develop a reputation as being one who gives thought to a particular subject. It is also okay to disagree with what is written as long as you follow the rule of thumb of disagreeing with the opinion of the person rather than the person.

There are ways to soften a response that differs from the writer such as "My experience has been a little different..."

To be a thought leader, or a leader of any type, you have to have followers. I am fond of a saying that goes "If you think that you are leading and you turn around and see no one is following you, then you are really just out for a walk." I think we all need to turn around every so often and see if anyone is following us.

We haven't answered the question yet of why we would even want to become a thought leader? Fame and fortune certainly would be nice, but on a smaller scale there is great value in becoming the "go to" person if a problem arises that you have the expertise to resolve.

I have been led to believe the media is always looking for experts on a specific subject. It would be great to be on a short list of experts the media reaches out to when they need a quote or sound bite on a topical subject. This is not only great attention for you, but it also raises attention for your business. It can be a great conversation starter. Can you imagine being able to respond to the question of "so... what's new?" with "Oh, I was on the Oprah show last week." We might have to settle with an interview by the local AM radio station, but you never know who is listening or what it might lead to.

Followers need leaders. If you lead, people will likely follow you. This can be an effective way to develop your business network. Get to know with your followers. Connect with them. Try it and see what happens. Let me know how your net's working.

BE THE RED CAR

At a recent networking event I commented to a woman that since having met her within the past year I was starting to see her at a lot of different events. She replied, "Yeah me to. You are the red car!"

I immediately recognized the red car reference from the Law of Attraction. The idea being if you were to buy a red car or even were thinking about buying one, then you would start noticing red cars everywhere. The Universe recreates itself for you. Up until that point, red cars were not in your range of focus.

Now when it comes to business networking, it would be advantageous for you to become that red car, i.e. someone that others recognize easily.

One way to become more visible would be to attend local events that provide networking opportunities and working the room so you "touch" many people i.e. interact with them. If you attend an event regularly, people will get used to seeing you there. It could get to the point that if you aren't in attendance someone might say "I wonder where... is?"

If you are not comfortable with interacting in a face-to-face situation, cyberspace can be a good resource for you. Social media venues such as Twitter, Facebook & Linkedin offer plenty of opportunities to create an on-line persona. By joining on-line groups that are locally based, you can easily interact with business people who you might not meet at a networking event or in the normal course of operating your business.

Both Linkedin and Facebook allow you to post updates which can help to keep your name front and center. So, when you actually do meet them in person, you already have something in common to talk about.

I am very active on-line promoting my articles such as this one as well as my business and events that I am organizing. I also have quite a few websites I have created and maintain. This tends to provide lots of entries in Google. If for whatever reason somebody was researching me, they would have lots of info to sift through. This works as a promotional tool for me.

I was at a Chamber of Commerce event and a young woman came up to me and said, "I just had to meet you. You are everywhere!" She was referring to my presence on local social media venues. To her I had become the "red car." She was actively visiting local sites, and my name and photo were popping up everywhere.

I believe there is an accompanying assumption. If you are seen everywhere i.e. being the red car, you are obviously well-connected, you have something of value to share and it would be worthwhile getting to know you.

How do you become the red car? It could be blue or any other color if you don't care for red. If I had my way, it would be a bright school bus-yellow pickup truck. But since I don't own one and it's on my wish list, perhaps seeing someone else driving one might not be so appreciated.

I am a little leery about putting my thoughts about a new pickup truck out to the universe. The last time I did, I had a new truck within a week. All I had to do was hit some black ice, do a 360 degree turn-around, land in a ditch, have the wheels fall off and have the truck written off.

So if you do become someone's "red truck" use your power wisely!

POWER NETWORKING SECRET REVEALED!

Okay, if you are thinking that's a pretty bold statement to make, I would agree with you.

Any time you see the words 'secret' and 'revealed' together in the same sentence, I would advise caution. It's usually followed by a request for payment for the content of the secret to be revealed to you. I'm going to reveal the secret to you for free. After all, it was given to me at no charge.

The secret to being a power networker is ... [drum roll please] **ACTASIF**.

Say what?

Simply put, to be a *power networker* i.e. one who is effective in their networking activities, *act as if you already are successful.*

You may find it somewhat anticlimactic to hear this one word secret if you haven't heard the expression before. Another way of saying it would be "fake it until you make it." Or with a bit of a stretch it could be "mind over matter."

"Act as if it were impossible to fail." -- Dorothea Brande

Apparently your mind doesn't know the difference between imagining and reality. You would think it would. I'm sure if I acted upon some of my imaginings as though they were real, I could find myself in a lot of trouble.

So, if your mind doesn't know the difference and you have the idea you are going to be fearful or perhaps you expect the networking event to be extremely stressful, then guess what? It will be stressful and cause you to be afraid. On the other hand, if you go to the event feeling confident, perhaps with the attitude of whatever happens... happens, then you might achieve different results.

"The antidotes to fear and ignorance are desire and knowledge. Propel yourself forward by learning what you need to learn to do what you want to do." --- Brian Tracy

Any effective sports coach is using this technique extensively. They spend a lot of their time working with the athlete in having them envision every aspect of their performance in their minds long before the actual live event.

"Never let the fear of striking out get in your way". Babe Ruth, 1895-1948, American Baseball Player

If you are a Law of Attraction believer, this is an example of a self-fulfilling prophecy, or even an example of the adage "You create your own reality."

My first experience with the **ACTASIF** philosophy was in my early years in Toastmasters. Toastmasters International is the world's leading provider of inexpensive communication & leadership skills training. As a new speaker I found it stressful to stand at the front of the room, with everybody staring at me and being acutely aware of my own nervousness.

It surprised me to learn that even though I was shaking and fearful inside while delivering my presentation, it was not noticed by those watching and listening to me.

There is a difference between inner & outer states. Yet, I am sure we can all think of an example of a speaker that their outward appearance was one of terror, which would likely be a magnification of their interior state at the time.

What I learned was the power of imagery. Before my presentations I would stand at the front of the room or wherever my delivery area would be and I would envision myself being successful. In my mind I would see an audience hanging on every word I said. They were nodding in appreciation of the content I was delivering, and they were laughing profusely at all of my jokes. I was a success... even before I delivered the presentation.

When it came time to deliver my presentation live, it wasn't stressful because I had already delivered the presentation in my mind and was successful. I will admit that quite often the live presentations didn't go quite as wonderful as in my imagination or some of the humor fell flat, but it didn't create any undue stress for me.

"If you do not do the thing you fear, the fear controls your life." --- Brian Tracy

Every time you make a presentation, and survive it, which you are likely to do, you incrementally build your self-confidence. Self-confidence is somewhat like a bank account --- the more successes you have in life, the more is added to your self-confidence balance.

When you undertake an activity that requires self-confidence, you dig into your balance and you use some of it. Unlike a bank account, using up some of your balance actually causes your balance to increase. The more risks you take and successfully overcome, the more your self-confidence will increase. Unlike a bank account though, if you don't use it, you will lose it. Maintaining a healthy self-confidence level requires practice.

I have found this very same imagery technique i.e. ACTASIF to be successful when I attend networking events. Before going to the event, perhaps while I am driving there, I envision myself having good quality conversations with the people I meet where I am not the least bit nervous. I see myself making some new connections I can both provide value to and receive value in return.

I would challenge you to test this method. When preparing to attend a networking event you usually would experience anxiety over try imagining yourself being successful with your networking. Envision yourself having successful and rewarding conversations. Then when you are actually at the event, act as if you are successful. Don't forget, you already were successful in your mind. As Captain Jean Luc Picard from Star Trek Next Generation would say "Make it so!"

"Most people are paralyzed by fear. Overcome it and you take charge of your life and your world." --- Mark Victor Hansen

WHEN YOU READ LINKEDIN PROFILES WHAT INFORMATION POPS OUT AT YOU - GOOD OR BAD?

My immediate response is to view their photo and their number of connections.

When I'm looking at their photo, I'm looking to see if it is professionally done. I don't care if they aren't photogenic, just that they have taken the time to upload a professional photo. If they can't do so, I would wonder about their professionalism.

For the most part, I don't accept invitations to connect from someone who hasn't taken the time to upload their professional photo, or any photo for that matter.

As for number of connections... I frequently get invitations from 3rd degree connections with less than 10 connections, from various parts of the world asking me to connect. I can only surmise Linkedin is providing them with possible people to connect with. I can't see how they would even see my name otherwise.

I don't connect with LIONs (Linkedin Open Networkers.) I don't believe they provide any value to me, and I don't want to be part of their bragging rights. In my opinion, with Linkedin, more isn't necessarily better.

Next, I look at what they have uploaded for their profile. As I am an author, writing about business networking, professional self-promotion and job-searching, among other topics, I look to see if they have written good promotional copy about themselves.

I look to see if it is written in 1st person or 3rd person. I look at their grammar and their literacy. I look for errors in their promotional copy that deters from their purpose. Example: a business consultant saying how they are the consummate details person, yet having several grammatical errors in their content. So much for being a details person. Worse yet, when I contacted them to point out the problem... no response. I'm not sure they provide value to me as a contact if they don't walk their talk.

I tend to be more analytical than the average person and had created an assessment tool I was using in my business to help professionals develop their Linkedin profiles.

HOW DO YOU DESCRIBE YOURSELF TO OTHERS AT A NETWORKING EVENTS WHEN YOU HAVE SEVERAL DIFFERENT ACTIVE CAREERS?

I have faced this challenge many times myself. As a registered nurse working in mental health as my main career, I've usually had several side-hustles on the go at the same time.

When I attend a business networking event, I'm usually there to promote one of my businesses or organizations I'm involved with rather than my nursing position.

In some of the books I have written I use a system I call 'how high does your elevator go?' The concept is buildings have elevators that go to different heights. Some may go to 2 floors, some may go to 20 floors. Some buildings may even have multiple elevators.

The concept when applied to using your elevator pitch is you come prepared with multiple elevator pitches, should the occasion to use some arise.

I also come prepared with multiple business cards. When attending a business networking event, I'm usually wearing a sports jacket and a dress shirt. I strategically place business cards for my different entities in each of my shirt, pants and sports jacket pockets so that I can readily offer them as needed.

What I would suggest is developing a one-size-fits all elevator pitch of yourself that describes you best. Then, when listening to the other person's elevator pitch, I would look for clues that allow you to interject with the other things you offer or your other roles.

The elevator pitch you choose to lead with should be appropriate for the setting you are attending. For example, I have served as a union representative with the role of helping my fellow workers with labor disputes. It would be inappropriate for me to introduce myself in a management setting as being a union person with the role of helping fight against management.

One thing to remember in an initial interaction with somebody you are meeting for the first time, your purpose is looking for common areas of interest. You're not trying to give them your complete life story or make a sale on the spot.

Your goal is to determine if there is enough reason to get together for further conversation, i.e. coffee chat, to explore commonalities.

TOP 15 NETWORKING NO-NO'S: POWER NETWORKING TIPS & TECHNIQUES

Throughout my publications I have provided tips & techniques to help improve your networking effectiveness. I thought it would be interesting and perhaps entertaining to take a look at the subject from a different perspective, i.e. what you really shouldn't do.

These aren't provided in any order of priority. See if you recognize any of them from your adventures in networking land.

1. No Show: (Not showing up for an appointment) When all is said and done it can be argued all you really own in life is your reputation. There are some people who don't respect other people's time. They make appointments they don't intend to keep, or they pre-empt the appointment for something more important than meeting with you. Soon they get the reputation of not being reliable or keeping commitments. Is this the reputation that you want to develop?

2. No Follow-up: (Not following up on something you said that you would do) BNI (Business Network International) founder Dr. Ivan Misner promotes the concept of 'givers gain.'

Offering to help someone with something or providing information that can help an individual move their business forward without expecting compensation is a good way to develop a network connection. Not following-up on what you said you were going to do takes away from your credibility and your reputation.

3. No Follow-up: (Not following through with contacting a connection) If you say you are going to follow-up with someone… do so. If you don't, at the least, you have missed an opportunity to develop a potential profitable connection. At the worst, well who knows!

4. Not focusing on your conversation partner, i.e. looking around the room for a better offer. I think we are guilty of this at one time or another. Let's face it, not everybody is all that interesting to listen to. And you know what… our conversation partner might be thinking the same thing about us! Listening is a skill.

You will find the more you listen to people, the more they think you are interested in them, the more they will reveal about themselves and they will think you are a fantastic conversationalist.

5. Sexist or racist language. I hear this far too often in conversations with people who should know better. It isn't acceptable, and I don't want to hear it.

6. Fly undone! Gents for heaven's sake check your fly when you leave the restroom. It might be a great conversation starter "So the bull's ready to get out is it?" But is this where you want the conversation to go? It can be challenging to recover from a position of embarrassment. Trust me I know. I was on stage for two hours once as an emcee with my fly undone.

7. I'm so wonderful! (Going on and on about yourself and not giving the other person a chance to talk) If you have been on the receiving end of listening to one of these types you will know that it is not fun. I would suggest hitting the Pause button and move on to the next opportunity.

8. Talking about someone else i.e. a third party who isn't part of the conversation in a derogatory manner. Some people are happiest when they are putting somebody else down. If you participate with someone like this, you are validating their behaviour and you will likely soon be labeled the same way. This is gossip.

9. Dump job: (Using your conversational partner as a sounding board without asking their permission to do so) We all have challenges in life, problems that are bothering us right now. It won't help your networking success rate if you become known as a whiner. That's what counselors are for.

10. Monopolizing the Other Person's Time. This is a little different from what is outlined in #7 I'm so Wonderful! If you are shy or uncomfortable with networking, it can be easy to stay with one person longer than you should. You are depriving both of you the opportunity to meet other people.

11. Disrespecting a Business Card: People tend to take their business card quite seriously. It is an extension of who they are. We aren't as serious about it as say the Japanese, however, picking your teeth with someone's business card is a not a great way to make friends and influence people.

12. Hit & Run: (Acting like a Shark) Sharks are a type of networker who go to a business networking event with the intent of making a sale right there, right now. They don't care about you or your business. They are only interested in what they can get from you. Don't be one! And don't allow yourself to be attacked by one either!

13. Not having Your Own Business Cards: This portrays the image you are not a serious networker. If you haven't even taken the time to develop and produce business cards to promote yourself, then why would I want to do business with you?

I have heard it said, "Oh I don't do business cards. I take the time to write their name down on a piece of paper with their contact information. It's more personal, and then I contact them with "hey remember me?" "Lame, lame, lame." That's all I can say about that comment.

14. Eating Food While Conversing: Many networking events offer food & beverage. Balancing a paper plate in one hand and a drink in the other can be challenging when reaching your hand out to shake another's.

My personal belief is if I'm eating, I will stand to the side and chow down, then when finished I will resume networking. I have had to stand an awfully long time with a plate of food in my hand, while listening to another to avoid appearing rude. Be careful of spinach dips. Spinach stuck to your teeth can take your conversational partner's focus to different directions than what you intended.

15. Networking While Inebriated: You are your own liquor control board. If you can't handle your liquor without getting mouthy, don't drink! What you say and do may come back to haunt you.

PART VI
PERSONAL DEVELOPMENT RESOURCE FILES

HOW BIG IS YOUR SANDBOX?

How big do goldfish grow? It seems an innocent enough question. The answer is "it depends."

It depends on the size of the aquarium they spend their days swimming around in. House-bound goldfish can perhaps make it to 2 to 3 inches. Goldfish that have been released to the wild and haven't ended up on the menu of somebody higher up the food chain have been reported to grow to a whopping 12 to 14 inches.

Unless you find the collecting of trivia to be fascinating, I would expect the next question forming in your mind to be "Who cares? Why is this important to me?" Okay, that was really two questions disguised as one...

The point: How many of us have had limitations placed upon our personal growth and development and our potential, by others or even worse... by ourselves?

In my high school years, I was excited about cooking and wanted to become a chef. After graduation, I found a position that would lead me towards achieving my goal. Or so I thought! It was my first foray into the working world, and I ended up having some very cynical and jaded older workers as my role models. If I wanted to survive in the workplace, I needed to be the same as them.

After a year of working as a cook's assistant, I experienced more than several people's shares of trouble and experienced a couple downward promotions. After a year working on the dishwasher in the Dietary Department in a large psychiatric facility, I wondered how low can you go? Then after a further demotion to the pot washer, I realized I guess you can go lower than a dishwasher. It was a hot and thoroughly nasty job.

My goal to becoming a chef vanished. I began to see myself as the 'boy from the kitchen.' I saw my future as perhaps becoming a Cleaner on the housekeeping staff or perhaps, if I was lucky, a position as Driver in the Transportation Department.

Each of those roles would have paid more money than I was making running a pot washer machine. The bar wasn't raised very high. I didn't have any long-term aspirations. As the saying goes, all my eggs were in one basket with the plan of becoming a chef. There was no plan B. I got caught up in the day-to-day activities of earning a living. I bought into the limitations others placed on me and those I had myself.

The game-changer for me was seeing a job posting on the bulletin board looking for Registered Nurses. It paid in excess of double the wages I was making as the Potwasher Supervisor. I had the requisite educational requirements and went off to college to achieve my diploma in nursing. I had broken free of the 'aquarium' that was limiting my growth. I was no longer the boy from the kitchen.

In an ironic twist of fate, I returned to the same facility five years later as a Registered Nurse and worked there for a decade, actually to the very day. Well, guess what? After a decade, I was finding the environment once again to be too small and restrictive to me. Once again, I was letting other people put restrictions and sanctions on me. Once again I was putting limits on what I could do.

As many others have done in the past, I took the geographical cure. I moved my family across the country to beautiful British Columbia, a new location where nobody knew me. A new life.

Twenty-five years ago I discovered the communications & leadership program at Toastmasters International, and in the beginning it took me a couple years to figure it out.

At about two years into the program, I was becoming frustrated. I wasn't growing. My fellow club members were able to provide me with an evaluation of my speech even before I delivered it. They were so used to my style they could predict how I would deliver a speech.

A fellow club member gave me some advice that I remember to this day. "Rae, you need a bigger sandbox." Simple, yet sage advice. For me to grow, I needed to experience opportunities that were outside of the comfort of my Toastmasters club. I needed to continually raise the bar on meeting challenges in life and accomplishing even more challenging, yet achievable goals.

Over the ensuing years I took on a series of leadership roles within Toastmasters... from club officers, to Area Governor, Division Governor, Lieutenant Governor of Education & Training and on to District Governor, Past District Governor, Division Governor and finally club President. A full circle that has provided me with increasing leadership challenges.

When I was a younger Toastmaster my mantra for fans of Conan the Barbarian, "That which doesn't kill you... makes you stronger!" Yes, it was quite cynical at the time. I have revised it to "That which challenges you... makes you stronger"

I have gone on from there to develop entrepreneurial pursuits and to lead community-based organizations. I have found I need an ever-increasing bigger sandbox.

I haven't forgotten about you dear reader. Is the size of your sandbox holding you back? Are the labels or sanctions others have placed on you holding you back? Do you have limiting beliefs holding you back from achieving anything or everything that you want in life?

It is close to New Years as I am writing this article. Many people are thinking about making New Year's resolutions. Is this the year you step out of your restrictive sandbox?

I would encourage you to visit a local Toastmasters club. The world needs more leaders. Toastmasters builds leaders. You can be one of them! As JoAnna McWilliams, Past President of Toastmasters International is often quoted as saying "If you get everything out of Toastmasters that you can get out of Toastmasters... you will never get out of Toastmasters!"

For this upcoming year... build yourself a bigger sand box. You will be glad you did.

TOP TEN PERSONAL EMPOWERMENT TIPS

Personal empowerment is something many of us take for granted, yet for others it is an elusive and difficult concept to grasp.

One definition of personal empowerment is "deriving the strength to do something through one's own thoughts and based on the belief that one knows what is best for oneself."

From a different perspective "a management practice of sharing information, rewards, and power with employees so that they can take initiative and make decisions to solve problems and improve service and performance."

"Empowerment is based on the idea that giving employees skills, resources, authority, opportunity, motivation, as well holding them responsible and accountable for outcomes of their actions, will contribute to their competence and satisfaction."

This article focuses on the former definition... *personal* empowerment. The latter sounds a little too condescending to me, and from my perspective usually comes with strings attached.

You will note while this document is targeted towards nurses, the information contained within is readily applicable to other healthcare providers and indeed anyone who wishes to increase their overall personal empowerment.

Note: As you read through this list of Personal Empowerment Tips you will note that while each skill set is independent of the others, it is also interdependent. Developing skills in one area will increase your effectiveness and skills in another, leading to your increased personal empowerment.

1. DEVELOP EFFECTIVE COMMUNICATION SKILLS.

Just because a person talks a lot, it doesn't mean that they are communicating. Communication is a two-way process. Person A sends a message to person B. If person B receives the message and understands it, then communication has taken place. At a time when effective oral communication skills are in high demand, we see a tendency for people to communicate electronically i.e. via e-mail rather than face-to-face communication. "You should have known. I sent you an e-mail on it!"

Effective communication skills include:

One to one communication, social & therapeutic (both taking your turn talking and listening to the other person);

- Written communication (e-mail, letters, blogs, web pages, memos) People will judge you on the way that you write.
- Nonverbal communication, i.e. body language. Learn to read other's and how your own body language is being presented. It can be helpful to ask another how they are interpreting your body language to see if it is congruent with how you thought you were communicating.
- Presentation skills.

I used to believe as nurses and healthcare providers we were in the service industry. Service as opposed to the sales industry, that is. But I was wrong. Yes, we provide basic and advanced healthcare services, but we are in sales every day. We are selling ourselves, our professional advice to our patients and their families, our expertise and our credibility.

Effective communication skills includes becoming good at public speaking, communicating interpersonally both orally and written, developing your listening skills and motivating others to take action or support your position. Presentations can be delivered in a 1-1 situation or with large groups of people.

2. DEVELOP YOUR LEADERSHIP SKILLS.

Skilled leaders are in demand in every progressive organization. There is a plethora of books on the subject as of late, but many fall short in giving you practical steps to develop your leadership skills.

Leadership can't be learned by osmosis. You learn to lead... by leading. Okay it's not that profound but many people have the mindset that to be the leader means you have to be the 'top person', 'the boss.' This isn't true!

Leadership skill development is a progressive, incremental process. Take advantage of every leadership opportunity that presents itself. They may seem to be small and rather simplistic, but will serve to develop your base skills so you can use those very same skills in more challenging situations.

If you think of an athlete practicing high jumping, you will see incremental skill development in action. Every time they are able to jump over the bar at a certain height, they celebrate and raise the bar a little higher. Leadership skill development works the same way, inch by inch. Leadership is about expanding your sphere of influence.

3. UNDERSTAND PERSONALITY TYPES.

As a leader, you will interact with people displaying different personality traits. Some will resonate with you and you will get along well with them. Others, like fingernails running down a chalkboard, will cause you great distress.

Psychologists and 'people that study people' have created personality classifications most people can be categorized by. Meyers-Briggs & True Colors being two systems that come readily to mind and are worth your time in researching them.

One doesn't need to be an expert at personality profiling, but a good understanding of "where a person is coming from" is helpful. Many of us have the tendency to personalize another's behavior toward us, example: "they are doing that on purpose just to annoy me!" It may be true, but perhaps not.

There is an adage from the mental health field "all behavior has meaning." It can be helpful in trying to determine what a person's behavior is trying to solve for them. Once you increase your understanding of the different personality types, you can further develop skills to work with them and help them to be more effective.

4. DEVELOP SYSTEMS THINKING SKILLS.

Peter Senge's **The Fifth Discipline: The Art & Practice of the Learning Organization** is a must read. The tools and ideas identified in this book are for destroying the illusion the world is created of separate, unrelated forces. We are all part of systems. Whether it be our family, our workplace or our place of worship, these are all examples of systems that are inter-related with yet other systems.

Systems-thinking makes sense of the dynamics in our lives. It identifies existing patterns. Once we learn to recognize them, we can seek the leverage point(s) that can resolve problems. There is a lot more going on in the world than the 'cause and effect' principle most of us are aware of.

5. DEVELOP ASSERTIVENESS SKILLS.

Assertiveness can be described as having your personal needs met but not at the expense of another's. Interpersonal relations that result in win-win positions can be enriching. There is a little more to it than making "I" vs "you" statements, but it really all begins with that basic concept. Taking personal responsibility for your feelings and expressing the effects that another's actions have upon you. "I feel this way when you..."

6. DEVELOP YOUR PERSONAL NETWORKING SKILLS.

The world is definitely getting smaller, as evidenced by the increase of on-line social networks such as Facebook, Linkedin & Twitter. The philosophy of six degrees of separation, as thought 100-150 years ago, is now down to three degrees.

If you haven't heard this one before it purports if you access your network for a question or a contact, you should be able to reach anyone in the world by connecting to a friend who is a friend of... who is a friend of. It may not work out that easily, but I guess it could happen or has happened. On-line connections can be readily made by requesting an 'invite' to join.

While on-line networking is increasing, old-fashioned face-to-face networking is every bit as important. Have you handed out any personal or business cards lately? Do you have any? You should! Don't forget to practice your hand shake!

7. DEVELOP YOUR PROBLEM SOLVING/CRITICAL THINKING SKILLS.

An argument I have often heard and participated in as well is that of "what is a nurse?"

It can be argued a nurse is a nurturer, we provide care, we give medication... "we treat the patient/client/consumer holistically." Yes, these are all true but the same argument can be forwarded by other healthcare disciplines. So what really makes a nurse?

I'm not sure if there is a definitive answer or if one is warranted for that matter. With my thirty-plus years of nursing experience, what truly defines a nurse to me is our advanced problem solving and critical thinking skills based on our specialized body of knowledge. True, we all know fellow nurses that those terms just don't seem to apply to them but I believe these two skills are vital for your survival and longevity as a nurse but more importantly for the successful caring of your patients.

8. PRACTICE STRESS RELIEF TECHNIQUES.

As in the expression "one man's junk is another man's treasure" the basis of the saying can be applied to the condition called 'stress.' What one person views as 'stressful' to the point of debilitation, another might find the exact situation 'invigorating!' I once knew a fellow nurse named Mary who was terrified to interact with a distraught client. Her hobby was skydiving! I know which option I would find less stressful.

We all experience stress though, one way or another. Each to their own, as the saying goes. How is it some seem to handle it better than others if not actually thriving on it? Some find yoga or meditating helpful. Counting to ten or ten thousand can help to reduce your anger in some anger-producing situations. I personally find having knowledge and experience on a particular matter can go a long way in preventing the stress from being created in the first place.

9. LEARN TO UNDERSTAND CHANGE MANAGEMENT PRINCIPALS.

It has often been said the only constant in life is change. It tends to cause a lot of stress in people and it is also often said people don't necessarily resist change, they resist being changed. Yes, change is a fact of life and there is a process behind it. If you understand the process, you can be an effective change agent and help minimize the effects on yourself and others.

10. DEVELOP YOUR MEETING SKILLS.

The busier life gets, the more we seem to have meetings. They are a fact of life. Sometimes it seems we are either in a meeting, thinking about going to another meeting, on our way to a meeting or wishing we were anywhere else but in this particular meeting.

You may have noticed by now that all the empowering skills forwarded so far are inter-related. 'Meeting skills' is a catch-all phrase to describe those skills needed to be effective as a meeting [group] leader or as a participant.

Well-developed meeting skills include knowing how to create an agenda and prepare minutes, an understanding of Roberts Rules of Order, how to handle a Question & Answer session, how to chair a meeting, how to make a presentation or a proposal to a committee etc. Meetings are an excellent venue to showcase your skills if you are seeking career advancement or if you are promoting or forwarding a cause.

THERE YOU HAVE WHAT I CONSIDER TO BE THE TOP TEN SKILLS THAT will empower you to make changes within your personal and your work-life. Changes that can open up new doors of opportunity. Changes that can improve the quality of your life and of others.

Which leads me to the big question... **"What are you going to do about it?"**

PART VII
JOB SEARCHING RESOURCES

SHOULD I BE HONEST ON LINKEDIN ABOUT BEING JOBLESS OR SHOULD I HIDE IT?

Should I be honest on LinkedIn about being jobless, or should I hide it?

In my observation, if you are honest on Linkedin about being jobless, the recruiters don't contact you and that feels very unfair. What is the best way to be honest but not punish yourself at the same time?

As originally answered on Quora.com...

I think your assertion may be a generalization. If you are not being contacted by recruiters, it may only mean you aren't on their radar. It doesn't necessarily mean they are snubbing you.

Linkedin provides a very good medium to promote one's experience, and more important, their abilities. Your entire Linkedin profile needs to be crafted to feature you as a solution to somebody's problem. Recruiters and employers search Linkedin for potential job/position candidates. They have a problem to solve, i.e. filling the position and they would likely want to generate a slate of possibilities, rather than just one individual.

One of the most powerful features of Linkedin is the area where you submit your name and your professional headline. As an example, here is mine: Rae Stonehouse Small Biz Consultant ☛ Speaker, Author, Speech/Presentations Coach, Power Networker & Toastmaster Extraordinaire. **Note:** This was active at the time of writing this article.

The theory is that if someone is looking for a Small Biz Consultant or a business consultant, my name would come up in their search. However, I just did a quick search under the term of Small Biz Consultant and didn't find that it was a popular listing, so I may have to readjust it somewhat.

The reason I bring this point up is I see too many people add their name, then something like 'looking for work'; 'out of work'; 'unemployed' or 'looking for opportunities.'

While this may be an honest approach, I believe it works against you. As the saying goes, "don't judge a book by its cover." People do all the time. The same applies to your Linkedin Name heading. If somebody reads your profile and sees something like 'unemployed', they are more likely to click through to the next person. You would be better listing what area of work you are looking for next to your name. Your professional headline is the next area that you want to craft to highlight your experience. Leave out the unemployed part, though.

Further down in your Linkedin profile under the Background/Summary section, you can further promote yourself. This is the area where you can effectively add you are between jobs and open to opportunities.

The original question refers to recruiters. There are many more people out there, besides recruiters, who may be in a position to help you in your job search. You need to get on their radar. Firstly, you need to develop a network of diverse connections. Don't necessarily limit yourself to people you actually know. Secondly, as stated earlier, you need to get on their radar.

One way to do this is to post articles you have written to your timeline, i.e. add an article link.

Your articles should place you as an expert, or at least a very experienced person on the particular subject. When Linkedin members view the posts and articles that come through on their feed, they filter it to their interests. Those who are interested and do click on your article are a possible resource for you. You won't know exactly who reads your articles but if they Like, share or comment, you can research them and connect if you haven't already.

Another technique is to upload your content to Slideshare, which is owned by Linkedin. It allows you to feature your work that puts you in a good light.

Yet another strategy that works for many people is to participate in Linkedin groups. By responding to posts you can set yourself up as a 'thought leader' on your subject of interest, which in turn can add to your exposure and connectedness.

Thanks for your question and good luck in your job search.

"If you are doing your best, you will not have to worry about failure." Robert S. Hillyer

Take your job seriously, but don't take their complaints personally. If you take it personally, you'll get upset and lose your edge. If you take it too personally, you'll lose your edge and your job. If you take it seriously... it's you with them. If you take it personally, it's you against them. What steps can you take to ensure keeping your cool?" Jeffrey Gitomer

HOW CAN YOU WRITE ON LINKEDIN THAT YOU WERE THE CREATOR OF A COMPANY'S DEPARTMENT?

How can you write on Linkedin that you were the creator of a company's department?

WALT WHITMAN, COWBOY POET (1819-1892) IS OFTEN QUOTED AS saying "If you done, it ain't bragging!"

The value of Linkedin is you can use it for your own personal marketing agency.

I have been led to believe people use Linkedin for three main reasons:

1. They are looking for work.

2. They need to hire somebody to work for them.

3. They have a problem to solve.

The content of your profile needs to be crafted so you come across as a solution to somebody's problem.

You comment, "it sounds very pretentious and not humble at all..."

For many of us, it can be challenging writing promotional content about ourselves. At first, it really felt awkward to me. I started learning how to do it by creating promotional copy for monthly events I was organizing for a local entrepreneurial society.

I took the same concept and applied it to my Linkedin profile and the About sections for all of my websites and Author Bios.

I've gone on to present workshops on **"Blow Your Own Horn: Personal Marketing & Promotion for Business Professionals,"** in my local community.

Once you get your head wrapped around the fact, you can and should post the experience, you need to decide whether you want to feature it i.e. so it is easily discoverable, or merely post it i.e. have it discoverable should the reader decide to drill down in your content.

A preliminary step before working on this particular section is to determine whether you want to promote yourself in the first person i.e. 'I did...' or the third person using me as an example "Rae did this..."

The next step is to sit down and create promotional content. The first step is to determine what the purpose is of stating the fact you have created a department. What do you hope to achieve? Are you hoping this will help you with future work searches? If so, go for it!

Then you need to determine what the important facts are, e.g.

· What was your role in creating this department?

· Did you have assistance, or did you really do it alone?

· Were there any seemingly insurmountable obstacles that you overcome?

· Were there any important lessons learned?

· Is the department still functional?

· Are you still a part of the new department, or have you moved on to other challenges?

· Are the organizational skills that you utilized in this project, transferable to other ones?

· Has there been any success stories or a demonstrable return on investment for the creation of this department?

Once you have created your promotional copy, you may need to edit it for size. While there seems to be lots of room to post your experience in Linkedin, you don't want to come across as too verbose.

You may also want to add impact to your Experience submission by including any documents, publications or graphics that can add to your message. You will want to make sure that you don't violate any copyright infringement or confidentiality issues, though.

If you can elicit any Testimonials from people who assisted with the development of the department or have benefited from it, it would be helpful for you to post them. It adds impact to your promotional copy. Then it becomes more than just you saying you did something.

Once you have completed and posted this section, I would encourage you to review the rest of your Linkedin profile. Is the section you just completed consistent with the other sections? Do you need to adjust your content in the other sections? Have you remained consistent with your person, i.e. first vs third?

FEEL FREE TO CHECK OUT MY LINKEDIN PROFILE AT HTTPS://CA. linkedin.com/in/raestonehouse/ to see how I have handled similar accomplishments.

ABOUT THE AUTHOR

Rae A. Stonehouse is a Canadian born author & speaker.

His professional career as a Registered Nurse working predominantly in psychiatry/mental health, has spanned four decades.

Rae has embraced the principal of CANI (Constant and Never-ending Improvement) as promoted by thought leaders such as Tony Robbins and brings that philosophy to each of his publications and presentations.

Rae has dedicated the latter segment of his journey through life to overcoming his personal inhibitions. As a 25+ year member of Toastmasters International he has systematically built his self-confidence and communicating ability. He is passionate about sharing his lessons with his readers and listeners.

His publications thus far are of the self-help, self-improvement genre and systematically offer valuable sage advice on a specific topic.

His writing style can be described as being conversational. As an author, Rae strives to have a one-to-one conversation with each of his readers, very much like having your own personal self-development coach.

Rae is known for having a wry sense of humour that features in his publications. To learn more about Rae A. Stonehouse, visit the Wonderful World of Rae Stonehouse at http://raestonehouse.com.

ALSO BY RAE A. STONEHOUSE

PROtect Yourself! Empowering Tips & Techniques for Personal Safety: A Practical Violence Prevention Manual for Healthcare Workers https://books2read.com/protectyourself

∼

Power of Promotion: On-line Marketing for Toastmasters Club Growth

https://books2read.com/powerofpromotion

∼

You're Hired! Job Search Strategies That Work (This is the complete program)

E-book & Paperback: https://books2read.com/yourehired

On-line E-course: (Available as a self-directed or instructor-led program) http://liveforexcellenceacademy.com/

∼

You're Hired! Resume Tactics: Job Search Strategies That Work

E-book & Paperback: https://books2read.com/resumetactics

On-line E-course: http://liveforexcellenceacademy.com/

∼

Job Interview Preparation: Job Search Strategies That Work

E-book & **Paperback:** https://books2read.com/jobinterviewpreparation

On-line E-course: http://liveforexcellenceacademy.com/

You're Hired! Leveraging Your Network: Job Search Strategies That Work

E-book & **Paperback:** https://books2read.com/leveragingyournetwork

On-line E-course: http://liveforexcellenceacademy.com/

You're Hired! Power Tactics: Job Search Strategies That Work (This is a box set containing the complete content of Resume Tactics, Job Interview Preparation & Leveraging Your Network)

E-book: https://books2read.com/powertactics

Power Networking for Shy People: How to Network Like a Pro

E-book & **Paperback:** https://books2read.com/networklikapronetworklikeapro

The Savvy Emcee: How to be a Dynamic Master of Ceremonies

E-book: The Savvy Emcee: How to be a Dynamic Master of Ceremonies E-book

Working With Words: How to Add Life to Your Oral Presentations is also available as an on-line course at https://liveforexcellenceacademy.com

If you have found this book and program to be helpful, please leave us a warm review wherever you purchased this book.

www.ingramcontent.com/pod-product-compliance
Lightning Source LLC
Chambersburg PA
CBHW030902080526
44589CB00010B/103